Chicken Tonight

s

ock
braries

D0318208

Good Housekeeping

Chicken Tonight

COLLINS & BROWN

First published in the United Kingdom in 2014 by
Collins & Brown
10 Southcombe Street
London
W14 0RA

An imprint of Anova Books Company Ltd

Copyright © The National Magazine Company Limited and
Collins & Brown 2014

All rights reserved. No part of this publication may be reproduced, stored in a
retrieval system, or transmitted in any form or by any means, electronic,
mechanical, photocopying, recording or otherwise, without the prior written
consent of the copyright holder.

The expression Good Housekeeping as used in the title of the book is the
trademark of the National Magazine Company and The Hearst Corporation
registered in the United Kingdom and USA, and other principal countries of the
world, and is the absolute property of The National Magazine Company and
The Hearst Corporation. The use of this trademark other than with the express
permission of The National Magazine Company or The Hearst Corporation is
strictly prohibited.

The Good Housekeeping website is
www.goodhousekeeping.co.uk

10 9 8 7 6 5 4 3 2 1

ISBN 978-1-909397-27-9

A catalogue record for this book is available from
the British Library.

Reproduction by Dot Gradations Ltd, UK
Printed and bound by 1010 Printing International Ltd, China

This book can be ordered direct from the publisher. Contact the marketing
department, but try your bookshop first.

www.anovabooks.com

Recipes in this book are taken from the Good Housekeeping recipe library and
may have been reproduced in previous publications.

Picture Credits

Photographers:
Neil Barclay (pages 11, 23, 37, 45, 52, 55,
56, 60, 61, 74, 75, 93, 137, 138, 151, 158,
161, 163, 168, 172, 179, 181, 185, 194
and 210); Martin Brigdale (pages 14, 140,
144, 147, 189, 205, 207, 212, 215 and
217); Nicki Dowey (pages 9, 12, 15, 17, 18,
19, 24, 25, 27, 30, 32, 35, 39, 40, 41, 46,
47, 48, 51, 54, 59, 63, 68, 69, 78, 81, 82,
84, 87, 88, 91, 92, 95, 98, 104, 114, 117,
118, 119, 121, 123, 124, 127, 128, 129,
130, 133, 134, 139, 45, 149, 150, 154,
156, 165, 169, 176, 180, 187, 188, 191,
199, 201, 203 and 216); Will Heap (pages
20 and 97); Gareth Morgans (page 111);
Craig Robertson (Basics photography and
pages 36, 42, 65, 70, 73, 83, 89, 94, 102,
105, 106, 107, 115, 143, 162, 173, 175,
177, 182, 184, 196, 198, 202, 206, 208,
211 and 213); Clive Streeter (page 157);
Lucinda Symons (pages 10, 31, 77, 79, 108,
109, 148, 171, 195 and 218).

Home Economists:
Anna Burges-Lumsden,
Joanna Farrow, Emma Jane Frost, Teresa
Goldfinch, Alice Hart, Lucy McKelvie, Kim
Morphew, Katie Rogers, Sarah Tildesley,
Jennifer White and Mari Mererid Williams.

Stylists:
Penny Markham, Lucy McKelvie, Wei Tang,
Helen Trent and Mari Mererid Williams.

Notes

Both metric and imperial measures are given for the recipes. Follow either set of measures,
not a mixture of both, as they are not interchangeable.
All spoon measures are level.
1 tsp = 5ml spoon; 1 tbsp = 15ml spoon.
Ovens and grills must be preheated to the specified temperature.
Medium eggs should be used except where otherwise specified.

Dietary Guidelines

Note that certain recipes contain raw or lightly cooked eggs. The young, elderly, pregnant
women and anyone with immune-deficiency disease should avoid these because of the slight
risk of salmonella.
Note that some recipes contain alcohol. Check the ingredients list before serving to children.

Contents

SOUPS

Leabharlanna Poiblí Chathair Bhaile Átha Cliath
Dublin City Public Libraries

Chicken & Mushroom Broth

Preparation Time 20 minutes • Cooking Time 20 minutes • Serves 4 • Per Serving 255 calories,
5g fat (of which 1g saturates), 16g carbohydrate, 1.4g salt • Dairy Free • Easy

4 skinless chicken breasts

Pesto (see Cook's Tips), made omitting the Parmesan

1.1 litres (2 pints) chicken stock (see page 222)

100ml (3½fl oz) medium sherry

150g (5oz) exotic mushrooms, cleaned and sliced

1 red chilli, seeded and halved (see Cook's Tips)

75g (3oz) conchigliette pasta

2 tbsp soy sauce

a small handful of chopped pak choi or spinach leaves

a dash of Tabasco to serve (optional)

1. Preheat the oven to 200°C (180°C fan oven) mark 6. Make a few slashes in the chicken breasts, then rub the pesto over the chicken, pushing it into the cuts. Put the chicken into a roasting tin and roast for 20 minutes.

2. Meanwhile, put the stock into a pan with the sherry and bring to the boil. Add the mushrooms, chilli and pasta. Cover the pan and simmer for 3 minutes until the pasta is cooked. Stir in the soy sauce.

3. Slice the chicken into the broth with the pak choi or spinach.

4. Ladle into warmed bowls and serve immediately. Add a dash of Tabasco if you like it hot.

COOK'S TIPS

• *Chillies vary enormously in strength, from quite mild to blisteringly hot, depending on the type of chilli and its ripeness. Taste a small piece first to check it's not too hot for you.*

• *Be extremely careful when handling chillies not to touch or rub your eyes with your fingers, as they will sting. Wash knives immediately after handling chillies for the same reason. As a precaution, use rubber gloves when preparing them if you like.*

• *Pesto*
Put a 20g pack roughly chopped basil into a food processor. Add 25g (1oz) finely grated Parmesan, 50g (2oz) pinenuts and 4 tbsp extra virgin olive oil and whiz to a rough paste. Alternatively, grind in a pestle and mortar. Season with salt and ground black pepper.

Coconut Broth & Chicken Noodles

Preparation Time 5 minutes • Cooking Time 15 minutes • Serves 4 • Per Serving 440 calories,
19g fat (of which 4g saturates), 42g carbohydrate, 1g salt • Easy

1 tbsp vegetable oil

2 tbsp tom yum (or Thai red curry)
   soup paste

900ml (1½ pints) hot chicken stock
   (see page 222)

400ml can unsweetened coconut
   milk

200g (7oz) thread egg noodles

2 × large boneless, skinless
   chicken breasts, cut into thin
   strips

350g (12oz) pack stir-fry vegetables

salt and ground black pepper

coriander leaves to garnish

prawn crackers to serve

1. Heat the oil in a large pan. Add the soup paste and fry for about 10 seconds. Add the hot stock and coconut milk and bring to the boil. Reduce the heat and simmer for about 5 minutes.

2. Meanwhile, cook the noodles in plenty of boiling water according to the pack instructions.

3. Add the chicken strips to the simmering soup and cook for 3 minutes. Add the stir-fry vegetables, mix well and season with salt and pepper.

4. Drain the noodles, then divide among four large warmed bowls and pour the soup on top. Garnish with the coriander and serve with prawn crackers.

Chicken Consommé

Preparation Time 30 minutes • Cooking Time 1¼ hours • Serves 4 • Per Serving 18 calories, 1g fat (of which trace saturates), 1g carbohydrate, 3.1g salt • Dairy Free • A Little Effort

- **1.7 litres (3 pints) well-flavoured fat-free chicken stock (see page 222)**
- **350g (12oz) skinless chicken breast, minced**
- **2 leeks, trimmed and thinly sliced**
- **2 celery sticks, thinly sliced**
- **2 carrots, thinly sliced**
- **2 shallots, diced**
- **2 medium egg whites, lightly whisked**
- **2 medium egg shells, crushed (see Cook's Tip)**
- **a dash of sherry or Madeira (optional)**
- **salt and ground black pepper**

1. Heat the stock in a pan. Combine the chicken and vegetables in another large pan, then mix in the egg whites and shells.

2. Gradually whisk in the hot stock, then bring to the boil, whisking. As soon as it comes to the boil, stop whisking, reduce the heat and simmer very gently for 1 hour. By this time, a crust will have formed on the surface and the stock underneath should be clear.

3. Carefully make a hole in the crust and ladle the clear stock out into a muslin-lined sieve over a large bowl. Allow to drain through slowly, then put back into the cleaned pan and reheat. Check the seasoning and flavour with a little sherry or Madeira, if you like.

COOK'S TIP
Egg shells and whites are used to make soups, such as consommé, clear. When heated slowly, they trap the impurities as they coagulate, forming a scum layer on the top of the soup. Once the layer of scum has formed, the soup is gently strained through kitchen paper or a cloth, leaving behind a clear soup.

Chicken & Bean Soup

Preparation Time 10 minutes • Cooking Time 30 minutes • Serves 4 • Per Serving 351 calories, 6g fat (of which 1g saturates), 48g carbohydrate, 2.7g salt • Dairy Free • Easy

1 tbsp olive oil

1 onion, finely chopped

4 celery sticks, chopped

1 red chilli, seeded and roughly chopped (see Cook's Tips, page 8)

2 boneless, skinless chicken breasts, about 125g (4oz) each, cut into strips

1 litre (1¾ pints) hot chicken (see page 222) or vegetable stock

100g (3½oz) bulgur wheat

2 × 400g cans cannellini beans, drained and rinsed

400g can chopped tomatoes

25g (1oz) flat-leafed parsley, roughly chopped

wholegrain bread and Hummus (see Cook's Tip) to serve

1. Heat the oil in a large heavy-based pan. Add the onion, celery and chilli and cook over a low heat for 10 minutes or until softened. Add the chicken strips and stir-fry for 3–4 minutes until golden.

2. Add the hot stock to the pan and bring to a simmer. Stir in the bulgur wheat and simmer for 15 minutes.

3. Stir in the cannellini beans and tomatoes and bring to a simmer. Ladle into four warmed bowls and sprinkle with chopped parsley. Serve with bread and hummus.

COOK'S TIP

Hummus

Soak 150g (5½oz) dried chickpeas overnight, then drain and rinse. Put into a large pan and cover with 600ml (1 pint) water. Bring to the boil, reduce the heat to a simmer and cook for 2½–3 hours until tender. Drain, reserving the liquid. Keep aside 2–3 tbsp chickpeas for garnishing. Put the remaining chickpeas into a blender with 2 large garlic cloves, the juice of 2 lemons, 75ml (2½fl oz) olive oil and 150ml (¼ pint) of the cooking liquid. Whiz to a purée. Add 150ml (¼ pint) tahini paste (sesame seed paste) and whiz to a soft dropping consistency. Sprinkle with olive oil, freshly chopped flat-leafed parsley and cayenne pepper or paprika to serve.

Chicken Noodle Soup

Preparation Time 30 minutes • Cooking Time 15 minutes • Serves 4 • Per Serving 229 calories,
7g fat (of which 1g saturates), 16g carbohydrate, 1.2g salt • Dairy Free • A Little Effort

1 tbsp olive oil
300g (11oz) boneless, skinless
  chicken thighs, cubed
3 garlic cloves, crushed
2 medium red chillies, seeded and
  finely diced (see Cook's Tips,
  page 8)
1 litre (1¾ pints) chicken stock
  (see page 222)

250g (9oz) each green beans,
  broccoli, sugarsnap peas and
  courgettes, sliced
50g (2oz) vermicelli or spaghetti,
  broken into short lengths
salt

1. Heat the oil in a large pan.
Add the chicken, garlic and chillies
and cook for 5–10 minutes until
the chicken is opaque all over.

2. Add the stock and bring to
the boil, then add the vegetables.
Reduce the heat and simmer for
about 5 minutes or until the
chicken is cooked through.

3. Meanwhile, cook the noodles
or pasta in a separate pan of
lightly salted boiling water for
about 5–10 minutes until al dente,
depending on the type of noodles
or pasta.

4. Drain the noodles or pasta, add
to the broth and serve immediately.

Leftover Roast Chicken Soup

Preparation Time 10 minutes • Cooking Time 45 minutes • Serves 4 • Per Serving 199 calories,
12g fat (of which 3g saturates), 12g carbohydrate, 0.1g salt • Gluten Free • Easy

3 tbsp olive oil
1 onion, chopped
1 carrot, chopped
2 celery sticks, chopped
2 fresh thyme sprigs, chopped
1 bay leaf
1 stripped roast chicken carcass
150–200g (5–7oz) cooked chicken,
  roughly chopped
200g (7oz) mashed or roast potato
1 tbsp double cream

1. Heat the oil in a large pan. Add the onion, carrot, celery and thyme and fry gently for 20–30 minutes until soft but not brown. Add the bay leaf, chicken carcass and 900ml (1½ pints) boiling water to the pan. Bring to the boil, then reduce the heat and simmer for 5 minutes.

2. Remove the bay leaf and chicken carcass and add the chopped cooked chicken and potato. Simmer for 5 minutes.

3. Put the soup into a food processor or blender and whiz until smooth, then pour back into the pan and bring to the boil. Stir in the cream and serve immediately.

Chicken Soup with Garlic & Parmesan Croûtons

Preparation Time 30 minutes • Cooking Time about 1¼ hours • Serves 6 • Per Serving 340 calories, 16g fat (of which 9g saturates), 26g carbohydrate, 0.3g salt • Easy

1 small chicken, about 1kg (2¼lb), cut into pieces
300ml (½ pint) dry white wine
a few black peppercorns
1–2 red chillies, seeded (see Cook's Tips, page 8)
2 bay leaves
2 fresh rosemary sprigs
1 celery stick, roughly chopped
4 carrots, 3 roughly chopped and 1 cut into fine matchsticks
3 onions, 2 quartered and 1 chopped
75g (3oz) pasta shapes
75g (3oz) butter, plus extra to grease
2 garlic cloves, crushed
1 cos lettuce, finely shredded
2 tbsp freshly chopped parsley
4 thick slices white bread
3 tbsp freshly grated Parmesan
salt and ground black pepper

1. Put the chicken pieces into a pan in which they fit snugly. Add the wine, peppercorns, chillies, bay leaves, rosemary and celery. Add the roughly chopped carrots, quartered onions and about 900ml (1½ pints) cold water, which should almost cover the chicken. Bring to the boil, reduce the heat, cover and simmer gently for 1 hour.

2. Leave to cool slightly, then transfer the chicken to a plate and strain the stock. When cool enough to handle, remove the chicken from the bones and tear into bite-size pieces. Put to one side.

3. Preheat the oven to 200°C (180°C fan oven) mark 6. Pour the stock into the pan. Bring back to the boil, then add the pasta and cook for 5 minutes.

4. Heat 25g (1oz) butter in a clean pan. Add the chopped onion and a crushed garlic clove and cook for 5 minutes until softened. Add the carrot matchsticks and cook for 2 minutes. Add the stock and pasta and cook for 5 minutes. Stir in the chicken, lettuce and parsley. Heat gently, stirring, until the lettuce has wilted. Season with salt and pepper.

5. Meanwhile, lightly grease a baking sheet. Mix together 50g (2oz) softened butter and the remaining garlic in a small bowl. Remove the crusts from the bread and spread the slices with the garlic butter, then sprinkle with Parmesan. Cut into squares and put on the prepared baking sheet, spacing them a little apart. Cook in the oven for 8–10 minutes until crisp and golden brown.

6. Serve the chicken soup with the hot garlic and Parmesan croûtons.

Cream of Chicken Soup

Preparation Time 10 minutes • Cooking Time 30 minutes • Serves 4 • Per Serving 398 calories,
12g fat (of which 6g saturates), 44g carbohydrate, 0.5g salt • Easy

3 tbsp plain flour
150ml (¼ pint) milk
1.1 litres (2 pints) home-made
    chicken stock (see page 222)
125g (4oz) cooked chicken, diced
1 tsp lemon juice
a pinch of freshly grated nutmeg
2 tbsp single cream
salt and ground black pepper
croûtons and fresh parsley sprigs
    to garnish

1. Put the flour into a large bowl, add a little of the milk and blend until it makes a smooth cream.

2. Bring the stock to the boil, then stir it into the blended mixture. Put back in the pan and simmer gently for 20 minutes.

3. Stir in the chicken, lemon juice and nutmeg and season to taste with salt and pepper. Mix the rest of the milk with the cream and stir in, then reheat without boiling.

4. Taste and adjust the seasoning. Ladle the soup into warmed bowls, sprinkle with croûtons and parsley sprigs and serve.

COOK'S TIP
Serve this smooth, rich soup with warmed bridge rolls, before a main course of plain roast or grilled meat.

Hearty Chicken Soup with Dumplings

Preparation Time 20 minutes • Cooking Time 40 minutes • Serves 4 • Per Serving 335 calories,
15g fat (of which 5g saturates), 31g carbohydrate, 0.3g salt • Easy

2 tbsp olive oil
2 celery sticks, roughly chopped
150g (5oz) carrots, roughly chopped
150g (5oz) waxy salad potatoes,
    thinly sliced
275g (10oz) chicken breast,
    thinly sliced
2 litres (3½ pints) hot chicken stock
    (see page 222)
75g (3oz) frozen peas
salt and ground black pepper
a handful of chives, roughly
    chopped, to garnish (optional)

FOR THE DUMPLINGS
100g (3½oz) plain flour
½ tsp baking powder
½ tsp salt
1 medium egg, well beaten
25g (1oz) butter, melted
a splash of milk

1. Heat the oil in a large pan.
Add the celery, carrots and
potatoes and cook for 5 minutes or
until the vegetables are beginning
to caramelise around the edges.
Add the chicken and fry for
3 minutes or until just starting
to turn golden. Pour in the hot
stock and simmer for 15 minutes,
skimming the surface occasionally
to remove any scum.

2. To make the dumplings, sift the
flour, baking powder and salt into
a bowl, then season with pepper.
Combine the egg, melted butter
and milk in a separate bowl, then
stir quickly into the flour to make
a stiff batter.

3. Drop half-teaspoonfuls of the
dumpling mixture into the soup,
then cover and simmer for a further
15 minutes.

4. Stir in the peas and heat
through. Check the seasoning,
sprinkle with pepper and serve
garnished with chives, if you like.

Thai Chicken & Noodle Soup

Preparation Time 20 minutes • Cooking Time about 30 minutes • Serves 4 • Per Serving 384 calories, 15g fat (of which 3g saturates), 36g carbohydrate, 2g salt • Dairy Free • Easy

vegetable oil for shallow- or
   deep-frying
225g (8oz) firm tofu, patted dry and
   cut into 1cm (½in) cubes
2.5cm (1in) piece fresh root ginger,
   peeled and finely chopped
2.5cm (1in) piece fresh or dried
   galangal, peeled and thinly sliced
   (optional, see Cook's Tip)
1–2 garlic cloves, crushed
2 lemongrass stalks, halved
   lengthways and bruised
1 tsp chilli powder
½ tsp ground turmeric
275g (10oz) cooked chicken, skinned
   and cut into bite-size pieces
175g (6oz) cauliflower, broken into
   small florets and any thick stems
   thinly sliced
1 large carrot, cut into matchsticks
600ml (1 pint) coconut milk
600ml (1 pint) chicken (see page
   222) or vegetable stock
a few green beans, trimmed and
   halved
125g (4oz) fine or medium egg
   noodles
125g (4oz) peeled prawns (optional)
3 spring onions, thinly sliced
75g (3oz) bean sprouts
2 tbsp soy sauce

1. Heat the oil in a wok or deep-fryer to 180°C (test by frying a small cube of bread; it should brown in 40 seconds). Fry the tofu, in batches, for 1 minute or until it is golden brown all over. Drain on kitchen paper.

2. Heat 2 tbsp oil in a large pan. Add the ginger, galangal, if using, garlic, lemongrass, chilli powder, turmeric and chicken pieces and cook, stirring for 2 minutes.

3. Add the cauliflower, carrot, coconut milk and stock or water. Bring to the boil, stirring all the time, then reduce the heat and simmer for 10 minutes. Add the beans and simmer for 5 minutes.

4. Meanwhile, bring a large pan of water to the boil and cook the noodles for about 4 minutes or according to the pack instructions. Drain the noodles and add them to the soup with the prawns, if using, the tofu, spring onions, bean sprouts and soy sauce. Simmer gently for 5 minutes or until heated through. Serve immediately.

COOK'S TIP

Dried galangal, which is similar in flavour to root ginger, needs to be soaked for 30 minutes before using. It is used chopped or grated in many Thai, Indonesian and Malay dishes.

Cock-a-Leekie Soup

Preparation Time 30–40 minutes • Cooking Time 1 hour 20 minutes • Serves 8 • Per Serving 280 calories, 4g fat (of which 1g saturates), 40g carbohydrate, 0.2g salt • Easy

1.4kg (3lb) oven-ready chicken
2 onions, roughly chopped
2 carrots, roughly chopped
2 celery sticks, roughly chopped
1 bay leaf
25g (1oz) butter
900g (2lb) leeks, trimmed and
sliced
125g (4oz) ready-to-eat dried
prunes, sliced
salt and ground black pepper
freshly chopped parsley to serve

FOR THE DUMPLINGS
125g (4oz) self-raising flour
a pinch of salt
50g (2oz) shredded suet
2 tbsp freshly chopped parsley
2 tbsp freshly chopped thyme

1. Put the chicken into a pan in which it fits quite snugly, then add the chopped vegetables, bay leaf and chicken giblets (if available). Pour in 1.7 litres (3 pints) water and bring to the boil, then reduce the heat, cover and simmer gently for 1 hour.

2. Meanwhile, melt the butter in a large pan. Add the leeks and fry gently for 10 minutes or until softened.

3. Remove the chicken from the pan and leave until cool enough to handle. Strain the stock and put to one side. Strip the chicken from the bones and shred roughly. Add to the stock with the prunes and softened leeks.

4. To make the dumplings, sift the flour and salt into a bowl. Stir in the suet, herbs and about 5 tbsp water to make a fairly firm dough. Lightly shape the dough into 2.5cm (1in) balls. Bring the soup just to the boil and season well. Reduce the heat, add the dumplings and cover the pan with a lid. Simmer for about 15–20 minutes until the dumplings are light and fluffy. Serve the soup sprinkled with chopped parsley.

COOK'S TIP
Make the stock a day ahead, if possible, then cool overnight. The following day, remove any fat from the surface.

Hot & Sour Soup

Preparation Time 20 minutes • Cooking Time about 35 minutes • Serves 4 • Per Serving 255 calories, 10g fat (of which 1g saturates), 19g carbohydrate, 0.7g salt • Dairy Free • Easy

1 tbsp vegetable oil

2 chicken breasts, about 300g (11oz), or the same quantity of tofu, cut into strips

5cm (2in) piece fresh root ginger, peeled and grated

4 spring onions, finely sliced

1–2 tbsp Thai red curry paste

75g (3oz) long-grain wild rice

1.1 litres (2 pints) hot weak chicken (see page 222) or vegetable stock

200g (7oz) mangetouts, sliced

juice of 1 lime

4 tbsp freshly chopped coriander to garnish

1. Heat the oil in a deep pan. Add the chicken or tofu and cook over a medium heat for 5 minutes or until browned. Add the ginger and spring onions and cook for a further 2–3 minutes. Stir in the curry paste and cook for 1–2 minutes to warm the spices.

2. Add the rice and stir to coat in the curry paste. Pour the hot stock or boiling water into the pan, stir once and bring to the boil. Reduce the heat, cover the pan and simmer for 20 minutes.

3. Add the mangetouts and cook for a further 5 minutes or until the rice is cooked. Just before serving, squeeze in the lime juice and stir to mix.

4. To serve, ladle into warmed bowls and sprinkle with the coriander.

Chicken & Chestnut Soup

Preparation Time 5 minutes • Cooking Time 45 minutes • Serves 4 • Per Serving 330 calories, 10g fat (of which 5g saturates), 52g carbohydrate, 0.2g salt • Gluten Free • Easy

25g (1oz) butter or margarine
1 large onion, chopped
225g (8oz) Brussels sprouts
900ml (1½ pints) chicken stock
  made from leftover carcass and
  any leftover chicken meat (see
  page 222)
400g can whole chestnuts, drained
2 tsp freshly chopped thyme or
  1 tsp dried thyme
salt and ground black pepper
chicken stock or milk to finish
fresh thyme sprigs to garnish

1. Melt the butter in a large heavy-based pan. Add the onion and fry gently for 5 minutes until softened.

2. Trim the sprouts and cut a cross in the base of each one. Add to the onion, then cover the pan with a lid and cook gently for 5 minutes, shaking the pan frequently.

3. Pour in the stock and bring to the boil, then add the remaining ingredients, with salt and pepper to taste. Reduce the heat, cover the pan and simmer for 30 minutes or until the vegetables are tender.

4. Leave the soup to cool a little, then transfer the soup in batches in a blender or food processor and whiz until smooth. Put back into the rinsed-out pan and reheat gently, then thin down with either stock or milk, according to taste.

5. Taste and adjust the seasoning. To serve, ladle into warmed bowls and garnish with thyme sprigs.

COOK'S TIP

Serve for an informal family lunch with hot garlic bread, wholemeal toast, cheese on toast or hot sausage rolls.

COOK'S TIP

Grilled Garlic Bread

Preheat the grill. Cut 1 large crusty loaf into 2cm (¾in) thick slices. Put 175g (6oz) cubed butter and 3 crushed garlic cloves into a small pan and heat gently until the butter has melted. Season with salt and pepper. Dip a bunch of stiff-stemmed thyme sprigs into the melted butter and brush one side of each slice of bread. Put the slices, buttered side down, on the grill rack. Cook for 1–2 minutes until crisp and golden. Brush the uppermost sides with the remaining butter, turn over and cook the other side. Serve immediately.

Chicken, Ham & Spinach Broth

Preparation Time 10 minutes, plus soaking • Cooking Time 16–20 minutes • Serves 4 • Per Serving 244 calories, 6g fat (of which 3g saturates), 32.5g carbohydrate, 1.7g salt • Gluten Free • Easy

125g (4oz) green or yellow split peas, soaked overnight in double their volume of cold water
25g (1oz) butter
225g (8oz) onions, chopped
1 tbsp ground coriander
40g (1½ oz) pearl barley
2 litres (3½ pints) ham or chicken stock (see page 222)
1 bouquet garni (see Cook's Tip)
225g (8oz) potatoes, cut into chunks
400g (14oz) carrots, cut into chunks
150g (5oz) each cooked chicken and ham, cut into chunks
150g (5oz) baby spinach leaves
salt and ground black pepper
fresh coriander sprigs to garnish
50g (2oz) finely grated Parmesan to serve (optional)

1. Drain the split peas, put into a pan and cover with cold water. Bring to the boil, then reduce the heat and simmer for 10 minutes. Drain the peas and discard the liquid.

2. Meanwhile, melt the butter in a pan. Add the onions and cook for 5 minutes or until soft but not coloured. Add the ground coriander and cook for 30 seconds.

3. Add the split peas, pearl barley, stock and bouquet garni to the pan. Bring to the boil, then reduce the heat and simmer for 40 minutes or until the peas and barley are tender. Add the potatoes and cook for 5 minutes, then add the carrots and cook for 5–10 minutes. Season to taste with salt and pepper.

4. Add the chicken, ham and spinach to the pan and bring back to the boil, then reduce the heat and simmer for 2–3 minutes. Ladle into warmed bowls, garnish with coriander sprigs, season with pepper and serve with grated Parmesan, if you like.

COOK'S TIP
To make a bouquet garni, tie together a sprig each of thyme and parsley with 1 bay leaf and 1 celery stick.

SALADS & LIGHT BITES

Chicken, Avocado & Peanut Salad

Preparation Time 15 minutes, plus chilling • Serves 4 • Per Serving 335 calories,
28g fat (of which 4g saturates), 2g carbohydrate, 0.1g salt • Gluten Free • Dairy Free • Easy

**2 roast chicken breasts, about
250g (9oz) total weight, skinned
and sliced**
75g (3oz) watercress
2 tbsp cider vinegar
1 tsp English ready-made mustard
5 tbsp groundnut oil

**1 large ripe avocado, halved,
stoned, peeled and thickly sliced**
**50g (2oz) roasted salted peanuts,
roughly chopped**
salt and ground black pepper

1. Arrange the sliced chicken on top of the watercress, cover with clingfilm and chill until ready to serve.

2. Put the vinegar, mustard and oil into a bowl, season with salt and pepper and whisk together. Add the avocado and gently toss in the dressing, making sure each slice of avocado is well coated.

3. Just before serving, spoon the avocado and dressing over the chicken and watercress. Sprinkle with the chopped peanuts and serve immediately.

Quick Chicken & Gruyère Salad

Preparation Time 15 minutes, plus chilling • Serves 8 • Per Serving 507 calories, 40g fat (of which 9g saturates), 7g carbohydrate, 0.7g salt • Gluten Free • Easy

900g–1kg (2–2¼lb) cooked, boned chicken, skinned and cut into bite-size pieces

4 celery sticks, thinly sliced

125g (4oz) Gruyère or Emmenthal cheese, coarsely grated

2 firm red apples, halved, cored and roughly chopped

125g (4oz) seedless black grapes, halved

200ml (7fl oz) olive oil

2 tbsp white wine vinegar

4 tbsp soured cream

4 tbsp mayonnaise

4 tbsp freshly chopped parsley

75g (3oz) toasted pecan nuts or walnuts

salt and ground black pepper

chopped coriander and rocket to serve

1. Put the chicken, celery, cheese, apples and grapes into a large bowl. Add all the other ingredients and toss well.

2. Adjust the seasoning, cover and leave to chill in the fridge for at least 10–15 minutes. Serve with chopped coriander scattered over the top and rocket.

COOK'S TIPS

• *Any strongly flavoured cheese can be used for this recipe. You could try crumbled Danish blue or blue Stilton.*

• *The whole salad can be completed the day before and kept covered in the fridge until required. Stir well before serving.*

Tarragon Chicken & Bean Salad

Preparation Time 15–20 minutes • Serves 4 • Per Serving 697 calories,
56g fat (of which 10g saturates), 18g carbohydrate, 1.6g salt • Easy

2 tbsp freshly chopped tarragon

2 tbsp freshly chopped flat-leafed parsley

1 tbsp olive oil

2 tbsp crème fraîche

200ml (7fl oz) mayonnaise

juice of ½ lemon

450g (1lb) cooked chicken, cut into bite-size pieces

400g can cannellini beans, rinsed and drained

50g (2oz) sunblush or sun-dried tomatoes

salt and ground black pepper

finely sliced spring onion to garnish

FOR THE SHALLOT DRESSING

2 tbsp sunflower oil

1 tsp walnut oil

2 tsp red wine vinegar

1 small shallot, very finely chopped

a pinch of caster sugar

1. Put the herbs into a food processor and add the olive oil. Whiz until the herbs are chopped. Add the crème fraîche, mayonnaise and lemon juice to the processor then season with salt and pepper. Whiz until well combined. (Alternatively, chop the herbs by hand, mix with the olive oil, then beat in the crème fraîche, mayonnaise, lemon juice and seasoning.) Toss the chicken with the herb dressing in a large bowl and put to one side.

2. To make the shallot dressing, whisk the ingredients together in a small bowl and season.

3. Tip the cannellini beans into a bowl, toss with the shallot dressing and season well. Arrange the cannellini beans in a serving dish. Roughly chop the tomatoes. Top the beans with the dressed chicken and tomatoes and garnish with finely sliced spring onion.

TRY SOMETHING DIFFERENT

• *Use 400g can mixed beans, chickpeas or red kidney beans instead of the cannellini beans.*

• *Replace the chicken with cooked turkey, cut into bite-size pieces.*

Chicken Caesar Salad

Preparation Time 15–20 minutes • Cooking Time 12 minutes • Serves 4 • Per Serving 498 calories, 31g fat (of which 9g saturates), 7g carbohydrate, 1.4g salt • Easy

2 tbsp olive oil

1 garlic clove, crushed

2 thick slices country-style bread, cubed

6 tbsp freshly grated Parmesan

1 cos lettuce, chilled and cut into bite-size pieces

700g (1½lb) cooked chicken breast, sliced

FOR THE DRESSING

4 tbsp mayonnaise

2 tbsp lemon juice

1 tsp Dijon mustard

2 anchovy fillets, very finely chopped

salt and ground black pepper

1. Preheat the oven to 180°C (160°C fan oven) mark 4. Put the oil, garlic and bread cubes into a bowl and toss well. Tip on to a baking sheet and cook in the oven for 10 minutes, turning halfway through.

2. Sprinkle the Parmesan over the croûtons and cook for 2 minutes or until the cheese has melted and the bread is golden.

3. Put all the dressing ingredients into a bowl, season with salt and pepper and mix.

4. Put the lettuce and sliced chicken into a bowl, pour the dressing over and toss. Top with the cheese croûtons.

Cheese Coleslaw with Roast Chicken

Preparation Time 15 minutes • Serves 4 • Per Serving 270 calories,
23g fat (of which 7g saturates), 8g carbohydrate, 0.6g salt • Gluten Free • Easy

**1 baby white cabbage, thinly
    shredded**
4 spring onions, finely chopped
1 large carrot, finely shredded
75g (3oz) mature Cheddar, grated
6 tbsp mayonnaise
ground black pepper
cress to garnish
sliced roast chicken to serve

1. Put the white cabbage, spring onions, carrot, cheese and mayonnaise into a large bowl and season with pepper.

2. Divide the coleslaw among four small bowls or plates and snip some cress over them. Serve with slices of roast chicken.

TRY SOMETHING DIFFERENT
• *Use either Gruyère or Emmenthal instead of Cheddar.*
• *Add freshly chopped chives or parsley.*
• *Sprinkle with 1 tbsp mixed seeds just before serving.*

Chargrilled Chicken Waldorf

Preparation Time 10 minutes • Cooking Time 16–20 minutes • Serves 4 • Per Serving 702 calories,
61g fat (of which 14g saturates), 10g carbohydrate, 1.9g salt • Gluten Free • Easy

125g (4oz) walnuts
olive oil to brush
2 skinless chicken breasts, about
  125g (4oz) each
100g (3½oz) salad leaves
125g (4oz) black seedless grapes
2 crisp, red apples, such as
  Braeburn, cored and thinly
  sliced

4 celery sticks, sliced into
  matchsticks
175g (6oz) Roquefort cheese, thinly
  sliced
150ml (¼ pint) mayonnaise
salt and ground black pepper
freshly chopped chives to garnish
  (optional)

1. Put the walnuts into a dry pan and toast over a medium-high heat, tossing regularly, for 2–3 minutes until golden brown. Set aside. Brush a griddle or frying pan with a little oil and put over a medium heat. Season the chicken with salt and pepper and cook for 8–10 minutes on each side or until cooked through. Put to one side.

2. Toss the salad leaves, grapes, apples, celery, walnuts and about two-thirds of the Roquefort together in a large bowl. Thickly slice the chicken and arrange on four plates with some salad.

3. Crumble the remaining cheese into the mayonnaise and mix well. Spoon 2 tbsp mayonnaise on to each plate, or serve separately, and garnish with chopped chives, if you like.

Zesty Orange, Chicken & Tarragon Salad

Preparation Time 15 minutes, plus chilling • Serves 4 • Per Serving 252 calories,
8g fat (of which 2g saturates), 20g carbohydrate, 0.5g salt • Gluten Free • Dairy Free • Easy

50g (2oz) pecan nuts or walnuts
350g (12oz) smoked chicken or
   cooked chicken breast, skinned
   and cut into long strips
2 oranges
2 small chicory heads

FOR THE DRESSING
grated zest and juice of 2 oranges
2 tbsp white wine vinegar
1 tsp caster sugar
5 tbsp olive oil
3 tbsp freshly chopped tarragon
1 large egg yolk
salt and ground black pepper

1. Put the nuts into a dry pan and toast over a medium-high heat, tossing regularly, for 2–3 minutes until golden brown. Chop roughly.

2. Whisk all the dressing ingredients together in a small bowl. Put the chicken strips into another bowl, spoon over the dressing, cover and chill for at least 1 hour.

3. Use a sharp knife to remove the peel and pith from the oranges, then cut into slices.

4. Put a layer of chicory into a large flat salad bowl, add the orange slices, then spoon the chicken and dressing over. Sprinkle the toasted nuts over the top and serve.

COOK'S TIPS
Instant flavour ideas for chicken
• *Snip bacon into a frying pan, cook until crisp and golden, then stir into warm, boiled new potatoes with shredded roast chicken and mustard mayonnaise. Serve with green salad.*
• *Roast a chicken with lots of tarragon, peppers, whole garlic cloves and olive oil. Serve with couscous, into which you've stirred the roasting juices.*
• *Pan-fry chicken breasts that have been marinating in olive oil with rosemary, thyme and crushed garlic. Serve with a fresh tomato sauce made by whizzing together ripe tomatoes, olive oil, basil and seasoning.*
• *Pan-fry chicken breasts in butter and put to one side. Add flaked almonds and pitted fresh cherries to the pan, toss over a high heat for 1–2 minutes and serve with the cooked chicken.*

Warm Chicken Liver Salad

Preparation Time 20 minutes • Cooking Time 8–10 minutes • Serves 4 • Per Serving 236 calories, 15g fat (of which 3g saturates), 3g carbohydrate, 0.8g salt • Gluten Free • Dairy Free • Easy

450g (1lb) chicken livers
1–2 tbsp balsamic vinegar
1 tsp Dijon mustard
3 tbsp olive oil
50g (2oz) streaky bacon rashers, rind removed, cut into small, neat pieces (lardons)

50g (2oz) sun-dried tomatoes or roasted red peppers, cut into thin strips
½ curly endive, about 175g (6oz)
100g (3½oz) rocket
1 bunch of spring onions, sliced
salt and ground black pepper

1. Drain the chicken livers on kitchen paper, then trim and cut into pieces.

2. To make the dressing, put the vinegar, mustard, 2 tbsp oil and salt and pepper into a small bowl. Whisk together and put to one side.

3. Fry the lardons in a non-stick frying pan until beginning to brown, stirring from time to time. Add the tomatoes or red peppers and heat through for 1 minute. Add the remaining oil and the chicken livers and stir-fry over a high heat for about 2–3 minutes until the livers are just pink in the centre.

4. Meanwhile, toss the endive, rocket and spring onions with the dressing in a large bowl. Divide among four plates, arrange the warm livers and bacon on top and serve at once.

Chicken with Bulgur Wheat Salad

Preparation Time 20 minutes, plus marinating • Cooking Time 30 minutes • Serves 4 •
Per Serving 429 calories, 12g fat (of which 1g saturates), 45g carbohydrate, 0.2g salt • Dairy Free • Easy

grated zest and juice of 1 lemon

4 skinless chicken breasts,
   about 125g (4oz) each, slashed
   several times

1 tbsp ground coriander

2 tsp olive oil

FOR THE SALAD

225g (8oz) bulgur wheat

6 tomatoes, chopped

½ cucumber, chopped

4 spring onions, chopped

50g (2oz) dried dates, chopped

50g (2oz) almonds, chopped

3 tbsp freshly chopped flat-leafed
   parsley

3 tbsp freshly chopped mint

salt and ground black pepper

1. Put half the lemon zest and juice into a bowl, then add the chicken breasts, coriander and 1 tsp oil. Toss well to mix. Leave to marinate while you prepare the salad. Preheat the grill to high.

2. To make the salad, cook the bulgur wheat for 10 minutes or according to the pack instructions. Put into a bowl, add the remaining salad ingredients and season well with salt and pepper. Add the remaining lemon zest, juice and oil and stir well.

3. Grill the chicken for 10 minutes on each side or until cooked through – the juices should run clear when the meat is pierced with a skewer. Slice the chicken and serve with the salad.

Basil & Lemon Chicken

Preparation Time 15 minutes, plus marinating • Serves 4 • Per Serving 331 calories,
25g fat (of which 5g saturates), 2g carbohydrate, 1.3g salt • Gluten Free • Dairy Free • Easy

**grated zest of 1 lemon, plus 4 tbsp
lemon juice**
1 tsp caster sugar
1 tsp Dijon mustard
175ml (6fl oz) lemon-infused oil
4 tbsp freshly chopped basil
2 × 210g packs roast chicken
250g (9oz) baby leaf spinach
**55g pack crisp bacon, broken into
small pieces**
salt and ground black pepper

1. Put the lemon zest and juice, sugar, mustard and oil into a small bowl and season with salt and pepper. Whisk together until thoroughly combined, then add the basil.

2. Remove any bones from the roast chicken, leave the skin attached and slice into four or eight pieces. Arrange the sliced chicken in a dish and pour the dressing over, then cover and leave to marinate for at least 15 minutes.

3. Just before serving, lift the chicken from the dressing and put to one side.

4. Put the spinach into a large bowl, pour the dressing over and toss together. Arrange the chicken on top of the spinach and sprinkle the bacon over the top. Serve at once.

Coronation Chicken

Preparation Time 20 minutes • Cooking Time about 50 minutes • Serves 6 • Per Serving 425 calories, 26g fat (of which 4g saturates), 14g carbohydrate, 0.6g salt • Easy

1 tbsp vegetable oil
1 onion, chopped
1 tbsp ground coriander
1 tbsp ground cumin
1½ tsp ground turmeric
1½ tsp paprika
150ml (¼ pint) dry white wine
500ml (18fl oz) chicken stock
   (see page 222)
6 boneless, skinless chicken
   breasts or thighs
2 bay leaves
2 fresh thyme sprigs
2 fresh parsley sprigs
salt and ground black pepper
3–4 tbsp freshly chopped flat-leafed
   parsley to garnish
mixed leaf salad and French bread
   to serve

FOR THE DRESSING

150ml (¼ pint) mayonnaise
5 tbsp natural yogurt
2 tbsp Mango Chutney
   (see Cook's Tip)
125g (4oz) ready-to-eat dried
   apricots, chopped
juice of ½ lemon

1. Heat the oil in a large heavy-based pan. Add the onion and fry for about 5–10 minutes until softened and golden. Add the spices and cook, stirring, for 1–2 minutes.

2. Pour in the wine, bring to the boil and let it bubble for 5 minutes to reduce right down. Add the stock and bring to the boil again.

3. Season the chicken with salt and pepper, then add to the pan with the bay leaves and herb sprigs. Cover and bring to the boil. Reduce the heat to low and poach the chicken for 25 minutes or until cooked through. Cool quickly by plunging the base of the pan into a sink of cold water, replacing the water as it warms up.

4. Meanwhile, to make the dressing, mix the mayonnaise, yogurt and mango chutney in a bowl. Drain the cooled stock from the chicken and whisk 200ml (7fl oz) into the mayonnaise mixture. Add the apricots and lemon juice and season well.

5. Slice the chicken into strips, then stir into the curried mayonnaise. Cover and chill until required. Sprinkle chopped parsley over the top and serve with a mixed leaf salad and French bread.

COOK'S TIP

Fresh Mango Chutney
To make 225g (8oz), you will need:
- *1 large ripe mango*
- *1 fresh green chilli, seeded (see Cook's Tips, page 8),*
- *juice of 1 lime*
- *¼ tsp cayenne pepper*
- *½ tsp salt*

Cut the mango in half lengthways, slicing either side of the large flat stone; discard the stone. Using the point of a knife, cut parallel lines into the mango flesh, almost to the skin. Score another set of lines to cut the flesh into squares. Turn the skin inside out so that the cubes of flesh stand up, then cut these off and place in a bowl.

Cut the chilli into fine rings and mix with the mango cubes, lime juice, cayenne and salt. Chill for 1 hour before serving. It will keep for up to two days in the fridge.

Easy Chicken Salad

Preparation Time 10 minutes • Serves 1 • Per Serving 323 calories, 18g fat (of which 5g saturates), 17g carbohydrate, 0.9g salt • Gluten Free • Dairy Free • Easy

100g (3½oz) shredded roast chicken, skin discarded
1 carrot, chopped
1 celery stick, chopped
¼ cucumber, chopped
a handful of ripe cherry tomatoes, chopped
1 tbsp Hummus (see Cook's Tip, page 13)
¼ lemon to serve

1. Put the chicken into a shallow bowl. Add the carrot, celery, cucumber and cherry tomatoes.

2. Top with the hummus and serve with lemon for squeezing over the salad.

TRY SOMETHING DIFFERENT

• *For an even more nutritious salad, add a few pumpkin seeds or sunflower seeds, or a handful of sprouted seeds such as alfalfa, or chopped watercress.*

• *For extra bite, add a little finely chopped red chilli; for extra sweetness, add some strips of red pepper.*

• *For extra flavour, add some chopped coriander or torn basil leaves.*

Orange & Chicken Salad

Preparation Time 15 minutes • Cooking Time 10 minutes • Serves 4 • Per Serving 252 calories, 8g fat (of which 2g saturates), 20g carbohydrate, 0.5g salt • Gluten Free • Dairy Free • Easy

50g (2oz) cashew nuts
zest and juice of 2 oranges
2 tbsp marmalade
1 tbsp honey
1 tbsp oyster sauce
400g (14oz) roast chicken, shredded
a handful of chopped raw
  vegetables, such as cucumber,
  carrot, red and yellow pepper
  and Chinese leaves

1. Put the cashew nuts into a dry frying pan over a medium-high heat and cook for 2–3 minutes, tossing regularly, until golden brown. Tip into a large serving bowl.

2. To make the dressing, put the orange zest and juice into the frying pan with the marmalade, honey and oyster sauce. Bring to the boil, stirring, then simmer for about 2–3 minutes until slightly thickened.

3. Add the roast chicken to the serving bowl with the chopped raw vegetables. Pour the dressing over the salad, toss everything together and serve immediately.

COOK'S TIP

Toasting the cashew nuts in a dry frying pan before adding them to the salad brings out their flavour, giving them an intense, nutty taste and a wonderful golden colour.

Quick Caribbean Chicken Salad

Preparation Time 10 minutes • Cooking Time 20 minutes • Serves 4 • Per Serving 543 calories, 33g fat (of which 6g saturates), 25g carbohydrate, 0.7g salt • Gluten Free • Dairy Free • Easy

chicken breasts, with skin, about 125g (4oz) each
4 tsp jerk seasoning
450g (1lb) Jersey Royal potatoes
100ml (3½fl oz) mayonnaise
2 tbsp wholegrain mustard
2 tbsp vegetable oil
1 red onion, cut into thin wedges
125g (4oz) brown-cap mushrooms, halved
225g (8oz) young spinach leaves
3 tbsp freshly chopped chives
lemon juice to taste
salt and ground black pepper

1. Preheat the grill to high. Season the chicken breasts with salt and pepper and rub with jerk seasoning. Grill the chicken breasts for about 5 minutes on each side or until cooked through. Put to one side.

2. Meanwhile, cook the potatoes in lightly salted boiling water for about 10 minutes or until tender. Drain, cool a little, then cut into chunks. Mix the mayonnaise and mustard together, then add to the potatoes, stir and put to one side.

3. Heat the oil in a large frying pan, add the onion and fry for 5 minutes. Add the mushrooms and cook for a further 2 minutes, then season with salt and pepper.

4. Combine the potato and mushroom mixtures in a bowl and add the spinach. Toss with the chives, add the lemon juice and season with salt and pepper. Cut the chicken into thick slices on the diagonal and serve with the salad.

Spring Chicken Salad with Sweet Chilli Sauce

Preparation Time 15 minutes, plus soaking • Cooking Time 10 minutes • Serves 4 • Per Serving 307 calories, 15g fat (of which 3g saturates), 8g carbohydrate, 0.2g salt • Gluten Free • Dairy Free • Easy

2 tbsp groundnut oil, plus extra to oil
4 boneless, skinless chicken breasts, each cut into four strips
1 tbsp Cajun seasoning (see Cook's Tip)
salt and ground black pepper

FOR THE SALAD
175g (6oz) small young carrots, cut into thin matchsticks
125g (4oz) cucumber, halved lengthways, seeded and cut into matchsticks
6 spring onions, cut into matchsticks
10 radishes, sliced
50g (2oz) bean sprouts, rinsed and dried
50g (2oz) unsalted peanuts, roughly chopped
1 large red chilli, seeded and finely chopped (see Cook's Tips, page 8)
2 tsp sesame oil
Thai chilli dipping sauce to drizzle

1. Soak eight bamboo skewers in cold water for 20 minutes. Oil a baking sheet.

2. Preheat the grill. Toss the chicken strips in the Cajun seasoning, then season with salt and pepper and brush with the groundnut oil. Thread on to the soaked skewers.

3. Place the skewered chicken strips on the prepared baking sheet and cook under the hot grill for about 3–4 minutes on each side until cooked through.

4. Place all the salad vegetables, peanuts and red chilli in a bowl, toss with the sesame oil and season well with salt and pepper.

5. Divide the vegetables among four serving plates, top with the warm chicken skewers and drizzle with the chilli sauce. Serve immediately.

COOK'S TIP
Cajun seasoning is a spice and herb mixture, which includes chilli, cumin, cayenne and oregano.

Warm Chicken Salad with Quick Hollandaise

Preparation Time 15 minutes • Cooking Time about 20 minutes • Serves 4 • Per Serving 411 calories, 34g fat (of which 19g saturates), 2g carbohydrate, 0.8g salt • Gluten Free • Easy

1 tbsp white wine vinegar

1 tbsp lemon juice

1 tbsp olive oil

3 chicken breasts, with skin, about 125g (4oz) each

150g (5oz) asparagus tips, trimmed

2 large egg yolks

125g (4oz) unsalted butter, melted

200g (7oz) baby salad leaves with herbs

salt and ground black pepper

lemon wedges to serve

1. Put the vinegar and lemon juice into a small pan over a medium heat. Bring to the boil, then lower the heat and simmer to reduce by half. Leave to cool slightly.

2. Heat a griddle until hot and brush with the oil. Put the chicken on a board, cover with clingfilm and gently flatten with a rolling pin. Remove the clingfilm, season with salt and pepper and griddle for about 8 minutes on each side or until cooked through. Keep warm.

3. Bring a large pan of lightly salted water to the boil. Cook the asparagus for 2–3 minutes until tender. Drain and keep warm.

4. Meanwhile, put the yolks in a blender and whiz for a few seconds until thickened. With the blender running, pour the reduced vinegar mixture slowly on to the eggs, then gradually add the melted butter – the mixture will start to thicken. If it's too thick, blend in a little hot water to loosen.

5. Cut the chicken into slices and divide among four plates with the asparagus and salad leaves. Serve with the hollandaise for drizzling and lemon wedges to squeeze over.

Warm Lentil, Chicken & Broccoli Salad

Preparation Time 20 minutes • Cooking Time 25 minutes • Serves 4 • Per Serving 332 calories, 16g fat (of which 3g saturates), 22g carbohydrate, 1.6g salt • Gluten Free • Dairy Free • Easy

125g (4oz) Puy lentils
225g (8oz) broccoli, chopped
1 large garlic clove, crushed
1 tsp English mustard powder
2 tbsp balsamic vinegar
4 tbsp olive oil
1 red pepper, seeded and sliced
    into rings
350g (12oz) smoked chicken breast,
    shredded
salt

1. Put the lentils into a pan and cover generously with boiling water. Cook for 15 minutes or until tender, or according to the pack instructions. Blanch the broccoli in a pan of boiling water for 2 minutes. Drain, refresh under cold water and put to one side.

2. Put the garlic into a bowl and use a wooden spoon to combine it with a pinch of salt until creamy, then whisk in the mustard, vinegar and 3 tbsp oil. Put to one side.

3. Heat the remaining oil in a frying pan, add the red pepper and cook for 5 minutes or until softened.

4. Add the chicken and broccoli and stir-fry for 1–2 minutes. Stir in the lentils and dressing and serve warm.

TRY SOMETHING DIFFERENT
• *Use smoked turkey or duck instead of smoked chicken.*
• *For extra flavour, add 2 fresh rosemary sprigs and 2 bay leaves when cooking the lentils, discarding them when you drain the lentils.*

Chicken & Salsa Verde Crostini

Preparation Time 20 minutes, plus chilling • Cooking Time 2 minutes • Makes 15 • Per Serving 208 calories, 9g fat (of which 1g saturates), 24g carbohydrate, 1.7g salt • Dairy Free • Easy

50g (2oz) walnuts
1 loaf walnut bread, cut into
    15 × 1cm (½in) slices
2 tbsp olive oil
1 tbsp sea salt flakes
175g (6oz) cooked chicken breast,
    thinly sliced
125g (4oz) sun-dried tomatoes in
    oil, drained and thinly sliced
fresh flat-leafed parsley leaves to
    garnish

FOR THE SALSA VERDE
3 tbsp each freshly chopped
    coriander, mint and basil
1 garlic clove, roughly chopped
2 tbsp Dijon mustard
3 anchovy fillets
1 tbsp capers
50ml (2fl oz) olive oil
juice of ½ lemon

1. Put the walnuts into a dry pan and toast over a medium-high heat, tossing regularly, for 2–3 minutes until golden brown. Chop finely and put to one side.

2. Put all the salsa verde ingredients into a food processor or blender and whiz until smooth. (Alternatively, use a pestle and mortar.) Cover and chill.

3. Preheat the grill to high. Put the bread on a baking sheet, brush with the oil and sprinkle with sea salt flakes. Grill for 1 minute on each side or until lightly toasted.

4. To serve, put two or three chicken slices on each crostini base, top with a spoonful of salsa verde and slices of sun-dried tomato, then garnish with a sprinkling of walnuts and flat-leafed parsley.

Chunky Pâté with Port & Green Peppercorns

Preparation Time 25 minutes, plus setting • Cooking Time about 1½ hours, plus cooling • Serves 8 •
Per Serving 344 calories, 22g fat (of which 8g saturates), 3g carbohydrate, 0.7g salt • Dairy Free • A Little Effort

**350g (12oz) boneless belly pork,
  rind removed, roughly chopped**
**1 large skinless chicken breast,
  about 150g (5oz)**
225g (8oz) chicken livers, trimmed
**1 large duck breast, about 200g
  (7oz), skinned and chopped into
  small pieces**
**125g (4oz) rindless streaky bacon
  rashers, diced**
3 tbsp port or brandy
1 tbsp freshly chopped rosemary
2 tbsp green peppercorns
salt and ground black pepper
crusty bread to serve

TO FINISH
a few bay leaves
2 tsp powdered gelatine
150ml (¼ pint) white port or sherry

1. Preheat the oven to 170°C (150°C fan oven) mark 3. Coarsely mince the belly pork in a food processor, retaining some small chunks. Mince the chicken breast in the processor, then mince the chicken livers.

2. Mix all the meats together in a large bowl with the port or brandy, 1 tsp salt, some pepper, the chopped rosemary and green peppercorns.

3. Pack the mixture into a 1.1 litre (2 pint) terrine and stand in a roasting tin containing 2.5cm (1in) boiling water. Cover with foil and cook in the oven for 1 hour.

4. Remove the foil and arrange a few bay leaves on top of the pâté. Cook for a further 30 minutes or until the juices run clear when the pâté is pierced in the centre with a sharp knife or skewer.

5. Drain the meat juices into a small bowl and leave to cool. Skim off any fat, then sprinkle over the gelatine and leave until softened. Stand the bowl in a pan of gently simmering water until the gelatine has dissolved. Stir in the port or sherry. Make up to 450ml (¾ pint) with water, if necessary.

6. Pour the jellied liquid over the pâté and chill until set. Store the pâté in the fridge for up to two days. Serve with crusty bread.

Chorizo Chicken

Preparation Time 10 minutes • Cooking Time 10 minutes • Makes 24 • Per Canapé 19 calories,
1g fat (of which trace saturates), trace carbohydrate, 0.3g salt • Gluten Free • Dairy Free • Easy

**200g (7oz) boneless, skinless
chicken breast, cut into
24 bite-size pieces**
100g (3½oz) thinly sliced chorizo
24 fresh sage leaves
12 cherry tomatoes, halved

1. Preheat the oven to 190°C
(170°C fan oven) mark 5. Spread
the chicken pieces on a board and
top each with a slice of chorizo, a
sage leaf and half a cherry tomato.
Secure with cocktail sticks.

2. Place on a baking sheet and
cook for 10 minutes or until the
chicken is cooked through.
Transfer the chicken and chorizo
skewers to a serving plate and
serve warm.

**TRY SOMETHING
DIFFERENT**
*Replace the chicken with 24 large
raw peeled prawns and cook for
5 minutes until the prawns turn pink.*

Easy Wrap

Preparation Time 10 minutes • Serves 4 • Per Serving 269 calories, 16g fat (of which 3g saturates), 17g carbohydrate, 1.7g salt • Easy

1 tsp salt

1 tsp ground black pepper

2 cooked chicken breasts, about 125g (4oz) each, cut into bite-size pieces

1 carrot, grated

1 avocado, halved, stoned, peeled and chopped

a small handful of rocket

juice of ½ lemon

3 tbsp mayonnaise

4 flour tortillas

1. Mix the salt with the pepper in a large bowl. Add the chicken, carrot, avocado and rocket and mix well.

2. In a separate bowl, mix the lemon juice with the mayonnaise, then spread over the tortillas. Divide the chicken mixture among the tortillas, then roll up and serve in napkins, if you like.

Lime & Chilli Chicken Goujons

Preparation Time 15 minutes • Cooking Time 20 minutes • Serves 4 • Per Serving 339 calories, 22g fat (of which 4g saturates), 22g carbohydrate, 1.9g salt • Easy

300g (11oz) boneless, skinless chicken thighs
50g (2oz) fresh breadcrumbs
50g (2oz) plain flour
2 tsp dried chilli flakes
grated zest of 1 lime
1 medium egg, beaten
2 tbsp sunflower oil
salt and ground black pepper
lime wedges to serve

FOR THE DIP
6 tbsp natural yogurt
6 tbsp mayonnaise
¼ cucumber, halved lengthways, seeded and finely diced
25g (1oz) freshly chopped coriander
juice of 1 lime

1. Put all the dip ingredients into a bowl. Season to taste with salt and pepper and mix well, then chill.

2. Cut the chicken into strips. Put the breadcrumbs into a bowl with the flour, chilli flakes, lime zest and 1 tsp salt and mix well. Pour the egg on to a plate. Dip the chicken in egg, then coat in the breadcrumbs.

3. Heat the oil in a frying pan over a medium heat. Fry the chicken in batches for 7–10 minutes until golden and cooked through. Keep each batch warm while cooking the remainder. Transfer to a serving plate, sprinkle with a little salt, then serve with the dip and lime wedges.

COOK'S TIP
For a lower-fat version, bake the goujons in the oven. Preheat the oven to 200°C (180°C fan oven) mark 6. Put the goujons on a lightly oiled baking sheet, brush each with a little oil and bake for 12–15 minutes until golden and cooked through.

Tangy Chicken Bites

Preparation Time 10 minutes • Makes 48 • Per Canapé 43 calories, 2g fat (of which 1g saturates), 4g carbohydrate, 0.1g salt • Easy

2 × 50g packs mini croustades
about 275g (10oz) fruity chutney,
such as mango (see page 44)
2 roast chicken breasts, skinned,
torn into small pieces
250g carton crème fraîche
a few fresh thyme sprigs

1. Place the croustades on a board. Spoon about ½ tsp chutney into each one. Top with a few shreds of chicken, a small dollop of crème fraîche and a few thyme sprigs. Transfer the croustades to a large serving plate and serve immediately.

TRY SOMETHING DIFFERENT
• Use mini poppadoms instead of croustades.
• Replace the fruity chutney with cranberry sauce.
• Instead of roast chicken, use turkey.

Throw-it-all-together Chicken Salad

Preparation Time 10 minutes • Serves 4 • Per Serving 215 calories, 9g fat (of which 2g saturates), 9g carbohydrate, 0.6g salt • Gluten Free • Dairy Free • Easy

4 chargrilled chicken breasts, about 125g (4oz) each, torn into strips
2 carrots, cut into strips
½ cucumber, halved lengthways, seeded and cut into ribbons
a handful of fresh coriander leaves, roughly chopped
½ head of Chinese leaves, shredded
4 handfuls of watercress
4 spring onions, shredded

FOR THE DRESSING
5 tbsp peanut butter
2 tbsp sweet chilli sauce
juice of 1 lime
salt and ground black pepper

1. Put the chicken strips and all the salad ingredients into a large salad bowl.

2. To make the dressing, put the peanut butter, chilli sauce and lime juice into a small bowl and mix well. Season with salt and pepper. If the dressing is too thick to pour, add 2–3 tbsp cold water, a tablespoon at a time, to thin it – use just enough water to make the dressing the correct consistency.

3. Drizzle the dressing over the salad, toss gently together and serve.

COOK'S TIPS
• *Use leftover roast chicken or beef, or cooked ham.*
• *Use washed and prepared salad instead of the Chinese leaves and watercress, if you like.*

OVEN-COOKED DISHES

Leabharlanna Poiblí Chathair Bhaile Átha Cliath
Dublin City Public Libraries

Glazed Chicken with Roast Lemons

Preparation Time 20 minutes • Cooking Time 1 hour 5 minutes • Serves 6 • Per Serving 340 calories, 5g fat (of which 2g saturates), 44g carbohydrate, 0.2g salt • Gluten free • Dairy free • Easy

250g (9oz) caster sugar
3 large lemons
6 chicken breast quarters
    (breast and wing) about 300g
    (11oz) each
salt and ground black pepper
fresh flat-leafed parsley to garnish

1. Put the caster sugar and 600ml (1 pint) water into a large pan and dissolve slowly over a low heat. Bring to the boil and bubble for 2 minutes. Pierce the skin of the lemons with a fork and put them into the sugar syrup, then cover and cook for 20 minutes.

2. Remove the lemons, bubble the liquid over a medium heat for about 12 minutes or until reduced by half and a golden caramel colour. Cut the lemons in half.

3. Preheat the oven to 230°C (210°C fan oven) mark 8. Season the chicken quarters with salt and pepper and put, skin side down, into a roasting tin that is just large enough to hold them in a single layer with the lemon halves. Pour the sugar syrup over the chicken and lemons.

4. Put the roasting tin on the middle shelf of the oven and cook for about 30–35 minutes or until cooked through. Baste the chicken from time to time and turn it over halfway through cooking.

5. Serve each piece of chicken with a lemon half (eat the flesh only, not the skin) and garnish with parsley.

Tarragon Chicken with Fennel

Preparation Time 10 minutes • Cooking Time 45–55 minutes • Serves 4 • Per Serving 334 calories, 26g fat (of which 15g saturates), 3g carbohydrate, 0.5g salt • Easy

1 tbsp olive oil
4 chicken thighs
1 onion, finely chopped
1 fennel bulb, finely chopped
juice of ½ lemon
200ml (7fl oz) hot chicken stock
  (see page 222)
200ml (7fl oz) crème fraîche
1 small bunch of tarragon,
  roughly chopped
salt and ground black pepper
new potatoes and broccoli to serve

1. Preheat the oven to 200°C (180°C fan oven) mark 6. Heat the oil in a large flameproof casserole over a medium-high heat. Add the chicken thighs and fry for 5 minutes or until browned, then remove and put them to one side to keep warm.

2. Add the onion to the casserole and fry for 5 minutes, then add the fennel and cook for 5–10 minutes until softened.

3. Add the lemon juice to the casserole, followed by the hot stock. Bring to a simmer and cook until the sauce is reduced by half.

4. Stir in the crème fraîche and put the chicken back into the casserole. Stir once to mix, then cover and cook in the oven for 25–30 minutes. Stir the tarragon into the sauce, season with salt and pepper and serve with potatoes and broccoli.

Chicken in Lemon Vinaigrette

Preparation Time 10 minutes • Cooking Time 40 minutes • Serves 6 • Per Serving 353 calories, 21g fat (of which 4g saturates), 10g carbohydrate, 0.3g salt • Gluten Free • Dairy Free • Easy

2 lemons
175g (6oz) shallots or onions, sliced
2 tbsp balsamic vinegar
2 tbsp sherry vinegar
4 tbsp clear honey
150ml (¼ pint) olive oil
6 boneless chicken breasts or
  12 boneless thighs, with skin
salt and ground black pepper
mashed potatoes to serve

1. Preheat the oven to 200°C (180°C fan oven) mark 6. Grate the zest and squeeze the juice of one lemon, then put to one side. Thinly slice the remaining lemon, then scatter the lemon slices and shallots or onions in a small roasting tin – it should be just large enough to hold the chicken comfortably in a single layer.

2. Whisk the lemon zest and juice, vinegars, honey and oil together in a bowl. Put the chicken into the roasting tin, season with salt and pepper and pour the lemon vinaigrette over it.

3. Roast in the oven, basting regularly, for about 35 minutes or until the chicken is golden and cooked through. Transfer the chicken to a serving dish and keep warm in a low oven. Put the roasting tin, with the juices, over a medium heat on the hob. Bring to the boil and bubble for 2–3 minutes until syrupy. Spoon over the chicken and serve with mashed potatoes.

GET AHEAD
To prepare ahead *Complete the recipe to the end of step 2, then cool, cover and chill for up to one day in a non-metallic dish. Transfer the chicken to a roasting tin before cooking.*
To use *Complete the recipe.*

Chicken with Peperonata Sauce

Preparation Time 20 minutes • Cooking Time 40 minutes • Serves 4 • Per Serving 383 calories, 17g fat (of which 4g saturates), 20g carbohydrate. 0.4g salt • Gluten Free • Dairy Free • Easy

2 onions, sliced

4 chicken legs

100ml (3½fl oz) dry white wine or chicken stock (see page 222)

1 tbsp vegetable oil

ground black pepper

new potatoes to serve

FOR THE PEPERONATA SAUCE

2 large red peppers, halved and seeded

2 large yellow peppers, halved and seeded

1 tbsp extra virgin olive oil

1 fat garlic clove, roughly chopped

1. Preheat the oven to 200°C (180°C fan oven) mark 6. Spread the onions over the base of a large roasting tin. Put the chicken legs on top, then pour 50ml (2fl oz) wine, water or stock over the chicken. Roast the chicken in the oven for 15 minutes, then brush with the vegetable oil to crisp up the skin, and season with pepper. Pour in the remaining wine if the onions are browning too quickly and roast for a further 25 minutes.

2. Meanwhile, make the peperonata sauce. Using a swivel-headed peeler, peel the peppers as thoroughly as you can. Apply as little pressure as possible, so you don't take off too much flesh under the skin. Cut the peppers into thin strips and put them into a frying pan with the olive oil. Cook over a medium heat for 5–7 minutes until they are just soft. Add the garlic for the last 2 minutes of cooking. Stir the peperonata sauce into the onions and cook for a further 5 minutes.

3. To serve, divide the chicken among four warm plates and serve with a spoonful of the peperonata sauce and steamed new potatoes.

Chicken Rarebit

Preparation Time 5 minutes • Cooking Time 25 minutes • Serves 4 • Per Serving 446 calories, 24g fat (of which 14g saturates), 9g carbohydrate, 1.3g salt • Easy

4 large chicken breasts, with skin, about 150g (5oz) each
15g (½oz) butter
1 tbsp plain flour
75ml (2½fl oz) full-fat milk
175g (6oz) Gruyère cheese, grated
00g (1oz) fresh white breadcrumbs
1 tsp ready-made English mustard
2 fat garlic cloves, crushed
1 medium egg yolk
boiled new potatoes and green beans to serve

1. Preheat the oven to 200°C (180°C fan oven) mark 6. Put the chicken in a single layer into an ovenproof dish and roast in the oven for 20 minutes or until cooked through.

2. Meanwhile, melt the butter in a pan over a low heat, then add the flour and stir for 1 minute. Gradually add the milk and stir to make a smooth sauce.

3. Add the cheese, breadcrumbs, mustard and garlic to the sauce and cook for 1 minute. Cool briefly, then beat in the egg yolk. Preheat the grill to medium-high.

4. Discard the skin from the cooked chicken and beat any juices from the dish into the cheese mixture. Spread the paste evenly over each chicken breast, then grill for 2–3 minutes until golden. Serve with new potatoes and green beans.

Herb Chicken with Roasted Vegetables

Preparation Time 15 minutes, plus marinating • Cooking Time 40 minutes • Serves 4 • Per Serving 453 calories, 29g fat (of which 7g saturates), 10g carbohydrate, 0.3g salt • Gluten Free • Dairy Free • Easy

2 garlic cloves
25g (1oz) fresh basil
25g (1oz) fresh mint
8 fresh lemon thyme sprigs
4 tbsp olive oil
4 whole chicken legs (drumsticks and thighs)
1 small aubergine, chopped
200g (7oz) baby plum tomatoes
2 red peppers, seeded and chopped
2 courgettes, sliced
juice of 1 lemon
salt and ground black pepper
green salad to serve

1. Whiz the garlic, two-thirds of the basil and mint and the leaves from 4 lemon thyme sprigs in a food processor, adding half the oil gradually until the mixture forms a thick paste. (Alternatively, use a pestle and mortar.)

2. Rub the paste over the chicken legs, then put into a bowl. Cover, then chill and leave to marinate for at least 30 minutes.

3. Preheat the oven to 200°C (180° fan oven) mark 6. Put the aubergine, plum tomatoes, red peppers and courgettes into a large roasting tin with the remaining oil and season with salt and pepper. Toss to coat. Add the chicken and roast in the oven for 30–40 minutes until the vegetables are tender and the chicken is cooked through.

4. Squeeze the lemon juice over the chicken and sprinkle over the remaining herbs. Serve immediately with a crisp green salad.

Oven-baked Chicken with Garlic Potatoes

Preparation Time 10 minutes • Cooking Time 1½ hours • Serves 6 • Per Serving 376 calories, 16g fat (of which 5g saturates), 32g carbohydrate, 1.2g salt • Easy

2 medium baking potatoes, thinly sliced
a little freshly grated nutmeg
600ml (1 pint) white sauce (use a ready-made sauce or make your own, see Cook's Tip)
½ × 390g can fried onions
250g (9oz) frozen peas
450g (1lb) cooked chicken, shredded
20g pack garlic butter, sliced
a little butter to grease
salt and ground black pepper
Granary bread to serve (optional)

1. Preheat the oven to 180°C (160°C fan oven) mark 4. Layer half the potatoes over the base of a 2.4 litre (4¼ pint) shallow ovenproof dish and season with the nutmeg, salt and pepper. Pour the white sauce over and shake the dish, so that the sauce settles through the gaps in the potatoes.

2. Spread half the onions on top, then scatter on half the peas. Arrange the shredded chicken on top, then add the remaining peas and onions. Finish with the remaining potatoes, arranged in an even layer, and dot with garlic butter. Season with salt and pepper.

3. Cover tightly with buttered foil and cook in the oven for 1 hour. Increase the heat to 200°C (180°C fan oven) mark 6, remove the foil and cook for 20–30 minutes until the potatoes are golden and tender. Serve with Granary bread, if you like, to mop up the juices.

COOK'S TIP

White Sauce

To make 600ml (1 pint) white sauce, melt 25g (1oz) butter in a pan, then stir in 25g (1oz) plain flour. Cook, stirring constantly, for 1 minute. Remove from the heat and gradually pour in 600ml (1 pint) milk, beating after each addition. Return to the heat and cook, stirring, until the sauce has thickened and is velvety and smooth. Season with salt, pepper and freshly grated nutmeg.

Orange & Herb Chicken

Preparation Time 10 minutes • Cooking Time 20–30 minutes • Serves 4 • Per Serving 180 calories, 4g fat (of which 1g saturates), 5g carbohydrate, 0.2g salt • Gluten Free • Dairy Free • Easy

125ml (4fl oz) orange juice
grated zest of 1 unwaxed orange
2 tbsp freshly chopped tarragon
2 tbsp freshly chopped flat-leafed parsley
1 tbsp olive oil

1 garlic clove, crushed
4 skinless chicken breasts, about 125g (4oz) each
4 small orange wedges
salt and ground black pepper
brown rice and watercress to serve

1. Preheat the oven to 200°C (180°C fan oven) mark 6. Whisk the orange juice, orange zest, herbs, oil and garlic together in a large bowl. Season with salt and pepper.

2. Slash the chicken breasts several times and put into a large ovenproof dish. Pour the marinade over them and top each chicken breast with an orange wedge.

3. Cook in the oven for 20–30 minutes until cooked through. Serve with brown rice and watercress.

Saffron Risotto with Lemon Chicken

Preparation Time 20 minutes • Cooking Time 30 minutes • Serves 4 • Per Serving 830 calories,
44g fat (of which 15g saturates), 50g carbohydrate, 0.9g salt • Gluten Free • Easy

zest and juice of 1 lemon
a small handful of fresh parsley
25g (1oz) blanched almonds
1 tbsp dried thyme
1 garlic clove
75ml (2½fl oz) olive oil
450ml (¾ pint) chicken stock
** (see page 222)**
4 boneless chicken breasts
** with skin**

50g (2oz) butter
225g (8oz) onions, finely chopped
a small pinch of saffron threads
225g (8oz) risotto (arborio) rice
125ml (4fl oz) white wine
50g (2oz) freshly grated Parmesan
salt and ground black pepper
fresh thyme leaves and lemon
** wedges to garnish**

1. Preheat the oven to 200°C (180°C fan oven) mark 6. Whiz the lemon zest, parsley, almonds, thyme and garlic in a food processor for a few seconds, then slowly add the oil and whiz until combined. Season with salt and pepper. Heat the stock in a pan to a steady low simmer.

2. Spread the lemon and herb mixture under the skin of the chicken. Put the chicken into a roasting tin, brush with 25g (1oz) melted butter and pour the lemon juice over it. Cook in the oven for 25 minutes, basting occasionally.

3. Meanwhile, make the risotto. Heat the remaining butter in a pan. Add the onions and fry until soft. Stir in the saffron and rice. Add the wine to the rice. Gradually add the hot stock, a ladleful at a time, stirring with each addition and allowing it to be absorbed before adding more. This will take about 25 minutes. Take the pan off the heat and stir in the Parmesan. Serve with the chicken, pouring any juices from the roasting tin over it. Garnish with thyme leaves and lemon wedges.

Simple Chicken

Preparation Time 5 minutes • Cooking Time about 25 minutes • Serves 4 • Per Serving 350 calories, 27g fat (of which 12g saturates), 0g carbohydrate, 0.3g salt • Gluten free • Easy

6 fresh tarragon sprigs
4 chicken breasts with skin
50g (2oz) butter, diced
4 garlic cloves, sliced
a little olive oil
ground black pepper
1 large glass of dry white wine
lightly crushed new potatoes and
   broad beans to serve

1. Preheat the oven to 220°C (200°C fan oven) mark 7. Push a sprig of tarragon under the skin of each chicken breast. Place skin side up, into a small roasting tin just large enough to hold the chicken comfortably.

2. Dot half the butter over the top, scatter the garlic over, drizzle with a little oil and season with pepper. Roast in the oven for 20–25 minutes until cooked through. The juices should run clear when the chicken is pierced with a skewer. Baste the chicken with the juices halfway through cooking.

3. Remove the chicken from the roasting tin and keep warm. Put the tin over a high heat and whisk in the wine, scraping up the sticky bits from the base of the tin.

4. While still bubbling, whisk the remaining butter into the sauce. Stir in the remaining tarragon. Divide the chicken among four plates and serve with the warm juices and lightly crushed new potatoes and broad beans.

Spicy One-pan Chicken

Preparation Time 5 minutes • Cooking Time 1 hour • Serves 1 • Per Serving 410 calories,
10g fat (of which 2g saturates), 51g carbohydrate, 0.9g salt • Dairy Free • Easy

½ red or white onion, sliced
½ yellow pepper, sliced
1 small parsnip, chopped
1 potato, cut into chunks
227g can chopped tomatoes
1 tbsp medium curry paste
150ml (¼ pint) hot vegetable stock
1 chicken leg
a little vegetable oil
salt and ground black pepper

1. Preheat the oven to 200°C (180°C fan oven) mark 6. Put all the vegetables into a roasting tin or ovenproof dish, together with the tomatoes. Stir the curry paste into the hot stock and pour over the vegetables. Season with pepper and cook in the oven for 30 minutes.

2. Put the chicken leg on top of the vegetables and drizzle with a little oil, then season with salt and pepper. Put the casserole back into the oven for 30 minutes until the vegetables are tender and the chicken is cooked and the juices run clear when the thickest part of the leg is pierced with a skewer.

Stuffed Chicken with Potatoes & Tomatoes

Preparation Time 10 minutes • Cooking Time 30–40 minutes • Serves 4 • Per Serving 488 calories, 25g fat (of which 11g saturates), 32g carbohydrate, 0.5g salt • Gluten Free • Easy

3 large potatoes, sliced
3 tbsp olive oil
4 chicken breasts with skin
125g (4oz) cream cheese with herbs
300g (11oz) cherry tomatoes on the vine
salt and ground black pepper

1. Preheat the oven to 220°C (200°C fan oven) mark 7. Line a roasting tin with baking parchment and spread the potatoes in the tin. Drizzle with 2 tbsp oil, toss to coat, then roast for 20–25 minutes.

2. Using a sharp knife, ease the skin away from each chicken breast, leaving it attached along one side. Spread the cream cheese across each breast, then smooth the skin back over it. Brush the skin with the remaining oil and season with salt and pepper.

3. Heat a non-stick frying pan over a medium heat until hot, add the chicken, skin side down, and fry for 5 minutes until browned. Carefully turn over and fry for 5 minutes on the other side.

4. Reduce the temperature to 190°C (170°C fan oven) mark 5. Put the chicken on top of the potatoes, add the tomatoes and roast for a further 10–12 minutes or until the chicken is cooked through. Serve with the potatoes and tomatoes.

Sticky Chicken Thighs

Preparation Time 5 minutes • Cooking Time 20 minutes • Serves 4 • Per Serving 218 calories,
12g fat (of which 3g saturates), 5g carbohydrate, 0.4g salt • Gluten Free • Dairy Free • Easy

1 garlic clove, crushed
1 tbsp clear honey
1 tbsp Thai sweet chilli sauce
4 chicken thighs
rice (optional) and green salad
to serve

1. Preheat the oven to 200°C (180°C fan oven) mark 6. Put the garlic into a bowl with the honey and chilli sauce and stir to mix. Add the chicken thighs and toss to coat.

2. Put the chicken into a roasting tin and roast in the oven for 15–20 minutes until golden and cooked through and the juices run clear when the thighs are pierced with a skewer. Serve with rice, if you like, and a crisp green salad.

TRY SOMETHING DIFFERENT

• *Try this with sausages instead of the chicken, if you like.*

• *Italian Marinade*
Mix 1 crushed garlic clove with 4 tbsp olive oil, the juice of 1 lemon and 1 tsp dried oregano. If you like, leave to marinate for 1–2 hours before cooking.

• *Oriental Marinade*
Mix together 2 tbsp soy sauce, 1 tsp demerara sugar, 2 tbsp dry sherry or apple juice, 1 tsp finely chopped fresh root ginger and 1 crushed garlic clove.

• *Honey and Mustard Marinade*
Mix together 2 tbsp grain mustard, 3 tbsp clear honey and the grated zest and juice of 1 lemon.

Stuffed Chicken Breasts

Preparation Time 5 minutes • Cooking Time 20 minutes • Serves 4 • Per Serving 297 calories,
13g fat (of which 7g saturates), trace carbohydrate, 1.4g salt • Gluten Free • Easy

vegetable oil to oil
150g (5oz) ball mozzarella
4 skinless chicken breasts, about
    125g (4oz) each
4 sage leaves
8 slices Parma ham
ground black pepper
new potatoes and spinach to serve

1. Preheat the oven to 200°C
(180°C fan oven) mark 6. Lightly oil
a baking sheet. Slice the mozzarella
into eight, then put two slices on
each chicken piece. Top each with
a sage leaf.

2. Wrap each piece of chicken in
two slices of Parma ham, covering
the mozzarella. Season with
pepper.

3. Put on the prepared baking
sheet and cook in the oven for
20 minutes or until the chicken is
cooked through. Serve with new
potatoes and spinach.

COOK'S TIP
*Sage has a strong, pungent taste,
so you need only a little to flavour
the chicken. Don't be tempted to
add more than just one leaf to each
chicken breast or it will overpower
the finished dish.*

Peppered Chicken with Orange

Preparation Time 5 minutes • Cooking Time 25 minutes • Serves 6 • Per Serving 464 calories,
28g fat (of which 14g saturates), 2g carbohydrate, 0.7g salt • Easy

6 chicken breast fillets with skin
1 tbsp olive oil
125g (4oz) butter, chilled
125g (4oz) onions, finely chopped
2 tsp peppercorns in brine
200ml (7fl oz) brandy
450ml (¾ pint) chicken stock
   (see page 222)
pared zest and juice of 1 large
   orange
salt and ground black pepper
fresh flat-leafed parsley sprigs to
   garnish
freshly cooked potatoes of your
   choice to serve

1. Preheat the oven to 180°C
(160°C fan oven) mark 4. Season
the chicken with plenty of pepper.

2. Heat the oil in a non-stick frying
pan. Add the chicken breasts and
cook for about 5 minutes until
golden. Put the chicken into an
ovenproof dish and cook in the
oven for about 20 minutes until
done.

3. Meanwhile, heat 25g (1oz) butter
in the pan. Add the onions and
peppercorns and cook, stirring,
for 10 minutes until golden and
soft. Add the brandy and bubble
to reduce by half. Add the stock,
pared orange zest and juice and
bubble again for about 7 minutes
to reduce by half.

4. Dice the remaining butter and
add a little at a time, whisking after
each addition. Season with salt and
pepper and keep warm.

5. Pour the sauce over the cooked
chicken, garnish with parsley and
serve with potatoes.

Chicken & Mushroom Pies

Preparation Time 20 minutes, plus chilling • Cooking Time 55 minutes–1 hour 5 minutes • Serves 4
Per Serving 805 calories, 58g fat (of which 14g saturates), 49g carbohydrate, 1.2g salt • Easy

2 tbsp olive oil

1 leek, about 200g (7oz), trimmed and finely sliced

2–3 garlic cloves, crushed

350g (12oz) boneless, skinless chicken thighs, cut into 2.5cm (1in) cubes

200g (7oz) chestnut mushrooms, sliced

150ml (¼ pint) double cream

2 tbsp freshly chopped thyme

500g pack puff pastry, thawed if frozen

plain flour to dust

1 medium egg, beaten

salt and ground black pepper

1. Heat the oil in a pan. Add the leek and fry over a medium heat for 5 minutes. Add the garlic and cook for 1 minute. Add the chicken and continue to cook for 8–10 minutes. Add the mushrooms and cook for 5 minutes or until all the juices have disappeared.

2. Pour the cream into the pan and bring to the boil. Cook for 5 minutes to make a thick sauce. Add the thyme, then season well with salt and pepper. Tip into a bowl and leave to cool.

3. Roll out the pastry on a lightly floured surface until it measures 33 × 33cm (13 × 13in). Cut into four squares. Brush the edges with water and spoon the chicken mixture into the middle of each square. Bring each corner of the square up to the middle to make a parcel. Crimp the edges to seal, leaving a small hole in the middle. Brush the pies with beaten egg, put on a baking sheet and chill for 20 minutes.

4. Preheat the oven to 200°C (180°C fan oven) mark 6. Cook the pies for 30–40 minutes until golden.

TRY SOMETHING DIFFERENT
For a vegetarian alternative, replace the chicken with 200g (7oz) cooked, peeled (or vacuum-packed) chestnuts, roughly chopped. Add another finely sliced leek and increase the quantity of mushrooms to 300g (11oz).

Chicken Kiev

Preparation Time 15 minutes, plus chilling • Cooking Time 45 minutes • Serves 6 • Per Serving 594 calories, 41g fat (of which 19g saturates), 20g carbohydrate, 1.2g salt • A Little Effort

175g (6oz) butter, softened
grated zest of ½ lemon
1 tbsp lemon juice
1 tbsp freshly chopped parsley
1 garlic clove, crushed
6 large boneless, skinless chicken
   breasts
25g (1oz) seasoned flour
1 medium egg, beaten
125g (4oz) fresh breadcrumbs
vegetable oil for deep-frying
salt and ground black pepper
potato wedges and peas to serve

1. Put the butter, lemon zest and juice, parsley, garlic and salt and pepper to taste into a bowl and beat well to combine. Alternatively, whiz in a food processor. Form into a roll, cover and chill for at least 1 hour.

2. Place the chicken breasts on a flat surface and, using a meat mallet or rolling pin, pound them to an even thickness. Cut the butter into six pieces and place one piece on the centre of each chicken breast. Roll up, folding the ends in to enclose the butter completely. Secure the rolls with wooden cocktail sticks.

3. Place the seasoned flour, beaten egg and breadcrumbs in three separate flat dishes. Coat each chicken roll with the flour, then turn them in the beaten egg and coat them with breadcrumbs, patting the crumbs firmly on to the chicken.

4. Place the rolls on a baking sheet, cover lightly with non-stick or greaseproof paper and chill in the fridge for 2 hours or until required, to allow the coating to dry.

5. Heat the oil in a deep-fryer to 160°C (test by frying a small cube of bread; it should brown in 60 seconds). Put two chicken rolls into a frying basket and lower into the oil. Fry for 15 minutes – the chicken is cooked when it is browned and firm when pressed with a fork. Do not pierce.

6. Remove the rolls from the fryer, drain on kitchen paper and keep them warm while you cook the remaining chicken. Remove the cocktail sticks before serving.

7. Serve with potato wedges. and peas.

TRY SOMETHING DIFFERENT
Spicy Chicken Kiev
To make the butter filling, sauté 1 finely chopped shallot with 2 tsp cayenne pepper in 1 tbsp butter until soft but not brown. Stir in 1 tbsp freshly chopped parsley. Combine with 175g (6oz) softened butter and season. Complete the recipe from step 2 as above.

Mediterranean Chicken

Preparation Time 5 minutes • Cooking Time 20 minutes • Serves 4 • Per Serving 223 calories, 7g fat (of which 1g saturates), 3g carbohydrate, 0.2g salt • Gluten Free • Dairy Free • Easy

1 red pepper, seeded and chopped

2 tbsp capers

2 tbsp freshly chopped rosemary

2 tbsp olive oil

4 skinless chicken breasts, about 125g (4oz) each

salt and ground black pepper

rice or new potatoes to serve

1. Preheat the oven to 200°C (180°C fan oven) mark 6. Put the red pepper into a bowl with the capers, rosemary and oil. Season with salt and pepper and mix well.

2. Put the chicken breasts into an ovenproof dish and spoon the pepper mixture over the top. Cook in the oven for 15–20 minutes until the chicken is cooked through and the topping is hot. Serve with rice or new potatoes.

TRY SOMETHING DIFFERENT
Use chopped black olives instead of the capers.

Chicken & Leek Filo Pie

Preparation Time 15 minutes • Cooking Time about 50 minutes • Serves 6 • Per Serving 331 calories, 18g fat (of which 10g saturates), 27g carbohydrate, 0.4g salt • Easy

- 75g (3oz) unsalted butter
- 2 large leeks, trimmed and finely sliced
- 2 large carrots, finely chopped
- 1 tbsp plain flour
- 400ml (14fl oz) hot chicken stock (see page 222)
- 2 tsp Dijon mustard
- 3 tbsp double cream
- 350g (12oz) cooked chicken (leftovers are fine), cut into chunks
- 2 tbsp freshly chopped parsley
- 12 sheets filo pastry, thawed if frozen
- salt and ground black pepper
- green salad to serve

1. Preheat the oven to 200°C (180°C fan oven) mark 6. Melt 25g (1oz) butter in a pan over a low heat. Add the leeks and carrots and cook for 15 minutes or until softened but not coloured. Stir in the flour and cook for 1 minute. Gradually add the hot stock, stirring constantly, until the sauce is smooth, then simmer for 10 minutes.

2. Stir in the mustard and cream and season with salt and pepper. Add the cooked chicken and chopped parsley and tip into a 1.7 litre (3 pint) ovenproof dish.

3. Melt the remaining butter in a small pan. Unroll the filo pastry and cover with a clean, damp teatowel. Put a single sheet on a board and brush with a little of the melted butter. Roughly scrunch up the pastry and put on top of the chicken mixture. Continue with the remaining filo until the top of the pie is covered.

4. Cook the pie in the oven for 20–25 minutes until the filo is golden and the chicken mixture is bubbling. Serve with a green salad.

GET AHEAD
To prepare ahead Complete the recipe to the end of step 2, but allow the sauce to cool completely before adding the chicken. Chill for up to two days or freeze for up to one month.
To use If frozen, thaw overnight at cool room temperature, then complete the recipe.

Easy Chicken & Ham Pie

Preparation Time 15 minutes • Cooking Time 30–35 minutes • Serves 6 • Per Serving 364 calories, 22g fat (of which 6g saturates), 17g carbohydrate, 1.1g salt • Easy

4 ready-roasted chicken breasts, shredded
100g (3½oz) cooked smoked ham, cubed
150ml (¼ pint) double cream
75ml (2½fl oz) chicken gravy
2 tbsp freshly chopped tarragon
1 tsp cornflour
½ tsp English mustard
250g (9oz) ready-rolled puff pastry
1 medium egg, beaten
ground black pepper

1. Preheat the oven to 200°C (180°C fan oven) mark 6. Put the chicken into a large bowl with the ham, then add the cream, gravy, tarragon, cornflour and mustard. Season with pepper and mix well.

2. Spoon into a shallow 1 litre (1¾ pint) baking dish. Unroll the puff pastry and position over the top of the dish to cover. Trim to fit the dish, then press the edges down lightly around the rim. Brush the egg over the pastry. Cook in the oven for 30–35 minutes until the pastry is golden and puffed up. Serve hot.

Chicken & Artichoke Pie

Preparation Time 20 minutes • Cooking Time 45 minutes • Serves 4 • Per Serving 241 calories, 9g fat (of which 5g saturates), 7g carbohydrate, 0.2g salt • Easy

3 boneless, skinless chicken breasts, about 350g (12oz)
150ml (¼ pint) dry white wine
225g (8oz) reduced-fat cream cheese with garlic and herbs
400g can artichoke hearts, drained and quartered
4 sheets filo pastry, thawed if frozen
olive oil to brush
1 tsp sesame seeds
salt and ground black pepper

1. Preheat the oven to 200°C (180°C fan oven) mark 6. Put the chicken and wine into a pan and bring to the boil, then cover, reduce the heat and simmer for 10 minutes. Remove the chicken with a slotted spoon and put to one side. Add the cheese to the wine and mix until smooth. Bring to the boil, then reduce the heat and simmer until thickened.

2. Cut the chicken into bite-size pieces, then add to the sauce with the artichokes. Season and mix well.

3. Put the mixture into an ovenproof dish. Brush the pastry lightly with oil, scrunch slightly and put on top of the chicken. Sprinkle with sesame seeds, then cook in the oven for 30–35 minutes until crisp. Serve hot.

TRY SOMETHING DIFFERENT
Replace the artichoke hearts with 225g (8oz) brown-cap mushrooms, cooked in a little water with some sea salt and pepper and lemon juice.

Chicken & Leek Pie

Preparation Time 15 minutes • Cooking Time 40–45 minutes • Serves 4 • Per Serving 591 calories, 23g fat (of which 15g saturates), 54g carbohydrate, 0.3g salt • Gluten Free • Easy

5 large potatoes, chopped into chunks
200g (7oz) crème fraîche
3 boneless chicken breasts, with skin, about 125g (4oz) each
3 large leeks, trimmed and chopped into chunks
about 10 fresh tarragon leaves, finely chopped
salt and ground black pepper

1. Preheat the oven to 200°C (180°C fan oven) mark 6. Put the potatoes into a pan of lightly salted cold water. Cover the pan and bring to the boil, then reduce the heat and simmer for 10–12 minutes until soft. Drain and put back into the pan. Add 1 tbsp crème fraîche, season with salt and pepper and mash well.

2. Meanwhile, heat a frying pan, add the chicken, skin side down, and fry gently for 5 minutes or until the skin is golden. Turn the chicken over and fry for 6–8 minutes. Remove the chicken from the pan and put on to a board. Tip the leeks into the pan and cook in the juices over a low heat for 5 minutes to soften.

3. Discard the chicken skin and cut the flesh into bite-size pieces (don't worry if it is not quite cooked through). Put the chicken back into the pan, stir in the remaining crème fraîche and heat for 2–3 minutes until bubbling. Stir in the tarragon and season with salt and pepper, then spoon into a 1.7 litre (3 pint) ovenproof dish and spread the mash on top.

4. Cook the pie in the oven for 20–25 minutes until golden and heated through. Serve hot.

TRY SOMETHING DIFFERENT

• *To use leftover chicken or turkey, don't fry the meat at step 2. Add it to the pan with the crème fraîche at step 3. Cook the leeks in 2 tsp olive oil.*

• *For a different flavour, make the mash with 2 large potatoes and a small celeriac, that has been peeled, cut into chunks and cooked with the potato.*

Chicken Pot Pies

Preparation Time 45 minutes • Cooking Time about 1 hour • Serves 4 • Per Serving 610 calories, 34g fat (of which 14g saturates), 47g carbohydrate, 1.2g salt • Easy

25g (1oz) butter

25g (1oz) plain flour, plus extra
    to dust

400ml (14fl oz) chicken stock
    (see page 222)

2 tbsp double cream

450g cooked chicken, shredded

100g (3½oz) each frozen peas and
    sweetcorn

2 tbsp freshly chopped parsley

275g (10oz) ready-made shortcrust
    pastry

plain flour to dust

1 medium egg, beaten

1. Melt the butter in a pan over a medium heat. Stir in the flour and cook for 1 minute, then remove from the heat and gradually blend in the stock. Cook over a gentle heat, stirring, until thickened. Simmer for 5 minutes, then add the cream and cook for 5 minutes.

2. Stir the chicken meat into the sauce with the peas, sweetcorn and parsley. Leave to cool a little.

3. Preheat the oven to 200°C (180°C fan oven) mark 6. Roll out the pastry on a lightly floured surface to 3mm (⅛in) thick. Use the top of a 300ml (½ pint) ovenproof basin as a guide and cut out four circles of pastry 2cm (¾in) larger than the diameter. Put to one side.

4. Divide the chicken mixture among four 300ml (½ pint) ovenproof basins. Dampen the edges of the pastry with water and use to top the basins, folding it over the edges. Cut a slit in the pastry to let out the steam and use the trimmings to decorate the pies, if you like. Brush with the beaten egg and bake in the oven for 30 minutes until golden on top and the filling is piping hot.

ROASTS

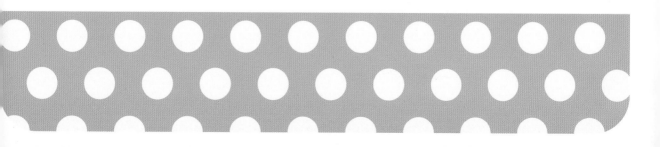

Roast Chicken with Stuffing & Gravy

Preparation Time 30 minutes • Cooking Time about 1 hour 20 minutes, plus resting • Serves 5 •
Per Serving 682 calories, 49g fat (of which 21g saturates), 17g carbohydrate, 1g salt • Easy

1.4kg (3lb) chicken
2 garlic cloves
1 onion, cut into wedges
2 tsp sea salt
2 tsp ground black pepper
4 fresh parsley sprigs
4 fresh tarragon sprigs
2 bay leaves
50g (2oz) butter, cut into cubes
salt and ground black pepper

FOR THE STUFFING
40g (1½oz) butter
1 small onion, chopped
1 garlic clove, crushed
75g (3oz) fresh white breadcrumbs
finely grated zest and juice of
   1 small lemon, halves reserved
   for the chicken
2 tbsp each freshly chopped
   flat-leafed parsley and tarragon
1 medium egg yolk

FOR THE GRAVY
200ml (7fl oz) white wine
1 tbsp Dijon mustard
450ml (¾ pint) hot chicken stock
   (see page 222)
25g (1oz) butter, mixed with 25g
   (1oz) plain flour (beurre manié,
   see Cook's Tip)

1. Preheat the oven to 190°C (170°C fan oven) mark 5. To make the stuffing, melt the butter in a pan, add the onion and garlic and fry for 5–10 minutes until soft. Cool, then add the remaining ingredients, stirring in the egg yolk last. Season well with salt and pepper.

2. Put the chicken on a board, breast upwards, then put the garlic, onion, reserved lemon halves and half the salt, pepper and herb sprigs into the body cavity.

3. Lift the loose skin at the neck and fill the cavity with stuffing. Turn the bird on to its breast and pull the neck flap over the opening to cover the stuffing. Rest the wing tips across it and truss the chicken. Weigh the stuffed bird to calculate the cooking time, and allow 20 minutes per 450g (1lb), plus an extra 20 minutes.

4. Put the chicken on a rack in a roasting tin. Season with the remaining salt and pepper, then top with the remaining herbs and the bay leaves. Dot with the butter and roast, basting halfway through, until cooked and the juices run clear when the thickest part of the thigh is pierced with a skewer.

5. Put the chicken on a serving dish and cover with foil. Leave to rest while you make the gravy. Pour off all but about 3 tbsp fat from the tin, put the tin over a high heat, add the wine and boil for 2 minutes. Add the mustard and hot stock and bring back to the boil. Gradually whisk in knobs of the butter mixture until smooth, then season with salt and pepper. Carve the chicken and serve with the stuffing and gravy.

COOK'S TIP
Beurre Manié
Beurre manié is a mixture of equal parts of softened butter and flour that has been kneaded together to form a paste. It is used to thicken sauces and stews and is whisked in towards the end of cooking, then boiled briefly to allow it to thicken.

Garlic & Rosemary Roast Chicken

Preparation Time 10 minutes • Cooking Time about 1 hour 20 minutes, plus resting • Serves 4–6 •
Per Serving 700–470 calories, 47–31g fat (of which 13–9g saturates), 18–12g carbohydrate, 2.3g salt • Easy

1.4kg (3lb) oven-ready chicken
4 tbsp freshly chopped rosemary or
    1 tbsp dried rosemary
450g (1lb) each red and yellow
    peppers, quartered and seeded
450g (1lb) courgettes, cut into
    wedges or halved lengthways
    if small
125g (4oz) pitted black olives
2 tbsp capers
2 garlic cloves
50ml (2fl oz) olive oil

125g (4oz) streaky bacon or pancetta
2 tsp cornflour
300ml (½ pint) white wine
300ml (½ pint) chicken stock
    (see page 222)
salt and ground black pepper
fresh flat-leafed parsley to garnish

1. Preheat the oven to 200°C
(180°C fan oven) mark 6. Fill the
chicken cavity with half the
rosemary.

2. Put the peppers, courgettes, black
olives, capers, garlic, oil and
seasoning into a roasting tin. Cover
the chicken with the remaining
rosemary, streaky bacon or pancetta
and sit it on the vegetables. Season
and cover the chicken with foil.

3. Cook in the oven for 1¼ hours,
removing the foil halfway through the
cooking time until the chicken is
cooked and the juices run clear when
the thickest part of the thigh is pierced
with a skewer.

4. Put the chicken and vegetables
on a warmed serving plate and cover
with foil. Leave the garlic in the
roasting tin with the cooking juices.

5. Mix the cornflour to a paste with
2 tbsp white wine. Add to the roasting
tin with the remaining wine, the stock
and seasoning, mashing the garlic into
the liquid with a fork. Bring to the boil,
stirring, then bubble for 5 minutes
or until lightly thickened. Adjust the
seasoning and serve with the chicken.
Garnish with parsley.

**TRY SOMETHING
DIFFERENT**
*Make with chicken breasts: prepare
peppers and courgettes as step 2; put
with the olives, capers, garlic and oil
into a roasting tin. Preheat the oven to
200°C (180°C fan oven) mark 6 and
cook for 30–35 minutes. Add six
chicken pieces. Snip the bacon and
sprinkle it over the portions with the
rosemary. Roast in the oven for
25–30 minutes. Remove the chicken
and vegetables. Complete the gravy
as steps 4 and 5.*

Pesto Roast Chicken

Preparation Time 10 minutes • Cooking Time about 1 hour 25 minutes, plus resting • Serves 4 •
Per Serving 715 calories, 58g fat (of which 14g saturates), 1g carbohydrate, 0.6g salt • Gluten Free • Easy

20g (¾oz) fresh basil, roughly chopped
25g (1oz) freshly grated Parmesan
50g (2oz) pinenuts
4 tbsp extra virgin olive oil
1.4kg (3lb) chicken
salt and ground black pepper
new or roast potatoes and green vegetables to serve

1. Preheat the oven to 200°C (180°C fan oven) mark 6. To make the pesto, put the basil, Parmesan, pinenuts and oil into a food processor and mix to a rough paste. (Alternatively, grind the ingredients using a pestle and mortar.) Season with salt and pepper.

2. Put the chicken into a roasting tin. Ease your fingers under the skin of the neck end to separate the breast skin from the flesh, then push about three-quarters of the pesto under the skin, using your hands to spread it evenly. Smear the remainder over the chicken legs. Season with pepper and roast in the oven for 1 hour 25 minutes or until the chicken is cooked and the juices run clear when the thickest part of the thigh is pierced with a skewer.

3. Put the chicken on a board, cover with foil and leave to rest for 15 minutes. Carve and serve with potatoes and green vegetables.

Mediterranean Roast Chicken

Preparation Time 40 minutes • Cooking Time about 1½ hours • Serves 4 • Per Serving 843 calories,
58g fat (of which 26g saturates), 42g carbohydrate, 0.9g salt • Gluten Free • Easy

900g (2lb) floury potatoes, such as Maris Piper, peeled and cut into chunks
125g (4oz) butter, softened
4 tbsp freshly chopped sage leaves, stalks reserved, plus extra leaves
4 tbsp freshly chopped thyme, stalks reserved, plus extra sprigs

1.4kg (3lb) chicken
juice of 1 lemon, halves reserved
2 fennel bulbs, cut into wedges
1 red onion, cut into wedges
salt and ground black pepper

1. Preheat the oven to 190°C (170°C fan oven) mark 5. Put the potatoes into a large pan of lightly salted cold water and bring to the boil. Cook for 5 minutes.

2. Meanwhile, put the butter into a bowl and mix in the chopped sage and thyme. Season well.

3. Put the chicken on a board and push the lemon halves and herb stalks into the cavity. Ease your fingers under the skin of the neck end to separate the breast skin from the flesh, then push the herby butter up under the skin, reserving a little. Season well.

4. Put the chicken into a large roasting tin, pour the lemon juice over it, then top with the extra sage and thyme and reserved butter. Drain the potatoes and shake in a colander to roughen their edges. Put around the chicken with the fennel and red onion. Roast in the oven for 1 hour 20 minutes or until the juices run clear when the thickest part of the thigh is pierced with a skewer. Carve and serve with the vegetables.

Spicy Roast Chicken with Red Peppers

Preparation Time 30 minutes • Cooking Time about 1½ hours • Serves 4 • Per Serving 787 calories, 49g fat (of which 11g saturates), 45g carbohydrate, 0.5g salt • Gluten Free • Dairy Free • Easy

900g (2lb) floury potatoes, such as Maris Piper, peeled and cut into chunks
2 tbsp sweet paprika
1 tbsp ground coriander
a large pinch of saffron threads, crushed
1 tsp each ground ginger and ground cinnamon
1 head of garlic, plus 2 crushed cloves

juice of ½ orange, plus 1 orange, cut into wedges
2 tbsp olive oil
1.4kg (3lb) chicken
1 small onion, halved
2 red peppers, seeded and cut into eighths
75g (3oz) pinenuts
salt and ground black pepper

1. Preheat the oven to 190°C (170°C fan oven) mark 5. Put the potatoes into a large pan of lightly salted cold water and bring to the boil. Cook for 5 minutes.

2. Meanwhile, put the paprika, coriander, saffron, ginger, cinnamon, 2 crushed garlic cloves, orange juice and oil into a bowl. Add ½ tsp each of salt and pepper and mix well. Put the chicken into a roasting tin and push the orange wedges and onion into the cavity. Season well, then rub the spice mix all over the chicken.

3. Drain the potatoes and shake in a colander to roughen their edges. Put around the chicken. Add the head of garlic and peppers and roast in the oven for 1 hour 20 minutes or until cooked.

4. About 10 minutes before the end of cooking, sprinkle the pinenuts over the chicken. Continue to cook until the juices run clear when the thickest part of the thigh is pierced with a skewer. Carve and serve with the vegetables.

Devilled Roast Chicken

Preparation Time 10 minutes • Cooking Time 1¼ hours, plus resting • Serves 4 • Per Serving 580 calories, 33g fat (of which 19g saturates), 31g carbohydrate, 1.3g salt • A Little Effort

2 tbsp olive oil
125g (4oz) onions, roughly chopped
2 red peppers, deseeded and
   roughly chopped
2 garlic cloves, crushed
1 tbsp Worcestershire sauce
1 tbsp cider vinegar
1 tsp dried marjoram
1 tsp dried thyme
2 tbsp dark muscovado sugar
300ml (½pint) lager
700g (1½lb) corn on the cob
400g can chickpeas, drained
   and rinsed
50g (2oz) butter, softened
2 tsp ground paprika
1.4kg (3lb) oven-ready chicken
salt

1. Preheat the oven to 200°C (180°C fan oven) mark 6. Heat the oil in a large roasting tin. Add the onions, peppers and garlic and fry, stirring, for 4–5 minutes until golden. Add the Worcestershire sauce, cider vinegar, marjoram, thyme, sugar and lager. Bring to the boil, reduce the heat and simmer for 5 minutes.

2. Cook the corn on the cob in a pan of lightly salted boiling water for 5–7 minutes, then strain, putting the cooking liquid to one side. Slice the corn on the cob thickly to remove the kernels. Add the corn and chickpeas to the roasting tin.

3. Mix together the butter, paprika and seasoning. Spread all over the chicken. Put the chicken into a large roasting tin, lying on one breast, and spoon over the corn mixture.

4. Cook for 1¼ hours until the juices run clear when the thickest part of the thigh is pierced with a skewer. After 20 minutes cooking, turn the chicken on to the other breast for 20 minutes, then on to its back for the remaining cooking time.

5. Put the chicken on a warmed plate and cover with foil. Pour off the excess fat and add 300ml (½ pint) reserved cooking liquid to the roasting tin. Bring the juices to the boil on the hob and bubble for 4–5 minutes. Adjust the seasoning and serve with the chicken.

TRY SOMETHING DIFFERENT
Make with chicken breasts: complete steps 1 and 2. Spread six chicken pieces with flavoured butter and put into a roasting tin on top of the sauce and corn mixture. Preheat the oven to 200°C (180°C fan oven) mark 6 and bake for 20–25 minutes until tender. Complete the sauce as in step 5.

Roast Chicken with Lemon & Garlic

Preparation Time 5 minutes • Cooking Time 1 hour–1¼ hours, plus resting • Serves 4 • Per Serving 639 calories, 46g fat (of which 13g saturates), 0g carbohydrate, 0.6g salt • Easy

1 chicken, about 1.8kg (4lb)
25g (1oz) butter, softened
2 tbsp olive oil
1½ lemons, cut in half
1 small head of garlic, cut in half horizontally
salt and ground black pepper
potatoes and seasonal vegetables to serve

1. Preheat the oven to 220°C (200°C fan oven) mark 7. Put the chicken into a roasting tin just large enough to hold it comfortably. Spread the butter all over the chicken, then drizzle with the oil and season with salt and pepper.

2. Squeeze lemon juice over the chicken, then put one lemon half inside the chicken. Put the other halves and the garlic into the roasting tin.

3. Roast the chicken in the oven for 15 minutes, then turn the heat down to 190°C (170°C fan oven) mark 5 and roast for a further 45 minutes–1 hour until the juices run clear when the thickest part of the thigh is pierced with a skewer. While the bird is cooking, baste from time to time with the pan juices. Add a splash of water to the tin if the juices dry out.

4. Put the chicken on a warmed plate, cover with foil and leave for 15 minutes, so that the juices that have risen to the surface can soak back into the meat. This will make it more moist and easier to slice. Mash some of the garlic into the pan juices and serve the gravy with the chicken. Serve with potatoes and seasonal vegetables.

Roast Curried Chicken

Preparation Time 20 minutes • Cooking Time 1½ hour plus resting • Serves 4 • Per Serving 650 calories, 37g fat (of which 18g saturates), 39g carbohydrate, 1.3g salt • A Little Effort

5cm (2in) piece fresh root ginger
1 whole chicken (weight about 1.8kg/4lb)
1 lime, halved
40g (1½oz) butter, softened
2 tbsp mild curry paste
000g (1¾lb) new potatoes, halved if large
¾ tbsp plain flour
165ml can coconut milk
1 tsp brown sugar (optional)
salt and freshly ground black pepper
seasonal vegetables to serve

1. Preheat the oven to 190°C (170°C fan oven) mark 5. Roughly chop half the ginger (leave the skin on) and put into the cavity of the bird. Add the lime halves and tie the legs together. Put the chicken into a large sturdy roasting tin. Put the butter and half the curry paste into a small bowl and mix together. Spread over the top and sides of the bird. Cover with foil and roast for 40 minutes.

2. Carefully remove the foil and add the potatoes to the tin, turning them to coat in the buttery mixture. Put back into the oven and cook for a further 40 minutes or until the potatoes are tender and the chicken is cooked through. Lift the chicken out of the tin and put on a board. Cover loosely with foil and leave to rest. Put the potatoes into a serving dish and keep warm.

3. Tilt the roasting tin and spoon off and discard most of the fat. Put the tin on the hob over a medium heat and stir in the flour and remaining curry paste, then grate in the remaining ginger. Stirring constantly, add the coconut milk. Fill the empty coconut can with water and add to the pan. Bring to the boil, then reduce the heat and simmer, stirring, for 3–5 minutes until thickened. Check the seasoning and add the sugar, if needed. Serve the chicken, roasted potatoes and gravy with seasonal vegetables.

GRILLS, PAN-FRIES, STIR-FRIES & PASTA

Garlic & Thyme Chicken

Preparation Time 10 minutes • Cooking Time 10–15 minutes • Serves 4 • Per Serving 135 calories, 6g fat (of which 1g saturates), trace carbohydrate, 0.2g salt • Gluten Free • Dairy Free • Easy

2 garlic cloves, crushed

2 tbsp freshly chopped thyme leaves, plus extra sprigs to garnish

2 tbsp olive oil

4 chicken thighs

salt and ground black pepper

1. Preheat the barbecue or grill. Mix the garlic with the chopped thyme and oil in a large bowl. Season with salt and pepper.

2. Using a sharp knife, make two or three slits in each chicken thigh. Put the chicken into the bowl and toss to coat thoroughly. Barbecue or grill for 5–7 minutes on each side until golden and cooked through. Garnish with thyme sprigs.

Chicken with Black-eye Beans & Greens

Preparation Time 5 minutes • Cooking Time 15 minutes • Serves 4 • Per Serving 491 calories, 26g fat (of which 4g saturates), 31g carbohydrate, 1.5g salt • Dairy Free • Gluten Free • Easy

2 tsp Jamaican jerk seasoning
4 skinless chicken breasts, about 125g (4oz) each
1kg (2¼lb) spring greens or cabbage, core removed and shredded
2 × 300g cans black-eye beans, drained and rinsed
8 tbsp olive oil
juice of 1¼ lemons
salt and ground black pepper

1. Preheat the grill. Rub the jerk seasoning into the chicken breasts and sprinkle with salt. Cook under the grill for 15 minutes or until cooked through, turning from time to time.

2. Cook the spring greens or cabbage in lightly salted boiling water until just tender – bringing the water back to the boil after adding the greens is usually enough to cook them. Drain and put back into the pan.

3. Add the beans and oil to the greens and season well with salt and pepper. Heat through and add the juice of 1 lemon.

4. To serve, slice the chicken and put on the bean mixture, then drizzle over the remaining lemon juice and serve immediately.

Grilled Chicken Breasts with a Cheese & Herb Crust

Preparation Time 15 minutes • Cooking Time 15 minutes • Serves 4 • Per Serving 600 calories, 53g fat (of which 11g saturates), trace carbohydrate, 1.4g salt • Easy

125g (4oz) olive oil bread, such as ciabatta, roughly chopped
75g (3oz) Gruyère cheese, grated
4 skinless chicken breast fillets, about 450g (1lb)
4 tbsp garlic mayonnaise or hollandaise sauce, plus extra to serve
4 tsp olive oil
salt and ground black pepper
fresh flat-leafed parsley to garnish
tomato salad to serve

1. Preheat the grill. Whiz the bread in a food processor until fine crumbs form. Transfer to a bowl, stir in the grated cheese and season well with salt and pepper.

2. Coat each chicken breast with 1 tbsp garlic mayonnaise or hollandaise, then dip in the crumbs until coated. Put on a baking sheet and drizzle each chicken breast with 1 tsp oil.

3. Cook the chicken under the hot grill, as far away from the heat as possible, for about 5–6 minutes on each side or until cooked through.

4. Slice the chicken, or leave whole, garnish with parsley and serve with a tomato salad and garlic mayonnaise or hollandaise.

COOK'S TIP
The crisp cheesy crumbs used for the crust keep the chicken breasts tender and moist as they cook under the grill.

Grilled Chicken with Pesto Butter

Preparation Time 10 minutes • Cooking Time 20–30 minutes • Serves 4 • Per Serving 340 calories, 23g fat (of which 12g saturates), trace carbohydrate, 0.6g salt • Gluten Free • Easy

4 skinless chicken breast fillets

75g (3oz) butter, softened

3 tbsp Pesto (see Cook's Tips, page 8)

lemon juice to sprinkle

salt and ground black pepper

freshly chopped parsley, to garnish

tomato salad, new potatoes and lemon wedges to serve

1. Make three or four deep cuts on each side of the chicken breasts. Season well with salt and pepper.

2. Put the butter into a bowl and gradually work in the pesto. Spread half of the pesto butter over the chicken and sprinkle with a little lemon juice.

3. Preheat the grill. Lay the chicken breasts on the grill rack and grill for about 10 minutes. Turn the chicken over, spread with the remaining pesto butter and sprinkle with a little more lemon juice. Grill for about 10 minutes or until cooked and the juices run clear when pierced with a skewer.

4. Serve the chicken on warmed plates, with any pan juices poured over, with tomato salad, potatoes and lemon wedges and garnished with chopped parsley.

Sticky Chicken Wings

Preparation Time 10 minutes, plus marinating (optional) • Cooking Time 20–45 minutes • Serves 4 •
Per Serving 257 calories, 14g fat (of which 4g saturates), 13g carbohydrate, 0.5g salt • Gluten Free • Dairy Free • Easy

4 tbsp clear honey

4 tbsp wholegrain mustard

12 large chicken wings

salt and ground black pepper

**grilled corn on the cob and green
salad to serve**

1. Put the honey and mustard into a large glass dish and mix together. Add the chicken wings and toss to coat. Season well with salt and pepper. Cook immediately or, if you've time, cover, chill and leave to marinate for about 2 hours.

2. Preheat the barbecue or grill. Lift the chicken from the marinade and cook for about 8–10 minutes on each side or until cooked through. Alternatively, roast in a preheated oven 200°C (180°C fan oven) mark 6 for 40–45 minutes. Serve hot, with grilled corn on the cob and a green salad.

TRY SOMETHING DIFFERENT

Hoisin, Sesame and Orange Marinade

Mix together 6 tbsp hoisin sauce, 1 tbsp sesame seeds and the juice of ½ orange. Add the chicken wings and toss to coat.

Middle Eastern Marinade

Mix together 3 tbsp harissa paste (see page 235), 1 tbsp tomato purée and 3 tbsp olive oil. Stir in a small handful each of freshly chopped mint and parsley, add the chicken wings and toss to coat.

Grilled Chicken with Mango Salsa

Preparation Time 10 minutes • Cooking Time 20 minutes • Serves 4 • Per Serving 288 calories, 14g fat (of which 4g saturates), 7g carbohydrate, 0.2g salt • Gluten Free • Dairy Free • Easy

4 chicken breasts
juice of ½ lime
oil-water spray (see Cook's Tip)
salt and ground black pepper
rocket to serve

FOR THE SALSA

1 mango, peeled, stoned and diced
1 small fennel bulb, trimmed and diced
1 fresh chilli, seeded and finely diced (see Cook's Tips, page 8)
1 tbsp balsamic vinegar
juice of ½ lime
2 tbsp freshly chopped flat-leafed parsley
2 tbsp freshly chopped mint

1. Preheat the grill. Put the chicken on a grill pan and season generously with salt and pepper. Sprinkle with the lime juice and spray with the oil-water blend. Grill for 8–10 minutes on each side until cooked through and the juices run clear when pierced with a skewer. Put to one side.

2. Combine all the salsa ingredients in a bowl and season generously with salt and pepper. Spoon alongside the chicken and serve with rocket.

COOK'S TIP

Oil-water spray is far lower in calories than oil alone and, as it sprays on thinly and evenly, you'll use less. Fill one-eighth of a travel-sized spray bottle with oil such as sunflower, light olive or vegetable (rapeseed), then top up with water. To use, shake well before spraying. Store in the fridge.

Chicken Tarragon Burgers

Preparation Time 30 minutes, plus chilling • Cooking Time 12 minutes • Serves 2 • Per Serving 205 calories, 4g fat (of which 1g saturates), 12g carbohydrate, 0.4g salt • Dairy Free • Easy

225g (8oz) minced chicken
2 shallots, finely chopped
1 tbsp freshly chopped tarragon
25g (1oz) fresh breadcrumbs
1 large egg yolk
vegetable oil to oil
salt and ground black pepper
toasted burger buns, mayonnaise
**   or Greek yogurt, salad leaves**
**   and tomato salad to serve**

1. Put the chicken into a bowl with the shallots, tarragon, breadcrumbs and egg yolk. Mix well, then beat in about 75ml (2½fl oz) cold water and season with salt and pepper.

2. Lightly oil a foil-lined baking sheet. Divide the chicken mixture into two or four portions (depending on how large you want the burgers) and put on the foil. Using the back of a wet spoon, flatten each portion to a thickness of 2.5cm (1in). Cover and chill for 30 minutes.

3. Preheat the barbecue or grill. If cooking on the barbecue, lift the burgers straight on to the grill rack; if cooking under the grill, slide the baking sheet under the grill. Cook the burgers for 5–6 minutes on each side until cooked through, then serve in a toasted burger bun with a dollop of mayonnaise or Greek yogurt, a few salad leaves and tomato salad

TRY SOMETHING DIFFERENT
Pork and Apricot Burgers
Replace the chicken with minced pork, use freshly chopped sage instead of tarragon, and add 100g (3½oz) chopped ready-to-eat dried apricots to the mixture before shaping.

Pancetta & Orange-wrapped Chicken

Preparation Time 30 minutes • Cooking Time 20–25 minutes • Serves 6 • Per Serving 374 calories,
21g fat (of which 7g saturates), 1g carbohydrate, 2.5g salt • Gluten Free • Dairy Free • Easy

2 garlic cloves

1 tsp sea salt

1 tsp freshly ground black pepper

2 tsp ground coriander

½ tsp ground cumin

**finely grated zest of 2 oranges plus
 juice of ½ orange**

**12 boneless, skinless chicken
 thighs**

12 thin slices pancetta

12 fresh bay leaves

olive oil

**Barbecued Red Peppers to serve
 (see Cook's Tip)**

1. Preheat the barbecue. Put the garlic, salt, pepper and spices into a small bowl and pound to a paste with the end of a rolling pin. (Alternatively, use a pestle and mortar.) Add the orange zest and juice and mix thoroughly.

2. Rub the paste over the chicken thighs. Carefully stretch the pancetta with the back of a knife. Put a bay leaf in the middle of each slice and put a thigh on top, smooth side down, then fold the ends of the pancetta over so they overlap in the middle. Make sure the bay leaf is well tucked in or it will burn during cooking.

3. Push a cocktail stick through each parcel to secure. Brush generously with oil. Barbecue for about 20–25 minutes, turning every 5 minutes until golden and cooked through. Serve drizzled with a little extra olive oil and barbecued red peppers.

COOK'S TIP
Barbecued Red Peppers
Halve 3 red peppers, remove the seeds, then cut into thick strips. Brush with 1 tbsp olive oil and season with salt and pepper. Cook on the barbecue or on a preheated griddle for 15–20 minutes until the peppers are tender.

Chicken Maryland

Preparation Time 30 minutes • Cooking Time about 20 minutes • Serves 4 • Per Serving 1307 calories, 72g fat (of which 20g saturates), 100g carbohydrate, 4.1g salt • Easy

3 tbsp seasoned flour
1 medium egg, beaten
125g (4oz) fresh breadcrumbs
1.4kg (3lb) chicken, jointed into
    fairly small pieces (see page 223)
25g (1oz) butter
3–4 tbsp vegetable oil

TO SERVE (see Cook's Tips)
Corn Fritters
4 Fried Bananas
4 Bacon Rolls

1. Place the seasoned flour, beaten egg and breadcrumbs in three separate flat dishes. Coat each chicken piece with flour, then turn them in the beaten egg and coat them with breadcrumbs, patting the crumbs firmly on to the chicken.

2. Heat the butter and oil in a large frying pan. Add the chicken and fry until lightly browned. Continue frying gently, turning the pieces once, for about 20 minutes or until tender. (Alternatively, heat vegetable oil in a deep-fryer to 190°C, test by frying a small cube of bread; it should brown in 20 seconds and deep-fry them for 5–10 minutes.)

3. Drain on kitchen paper, then serve with the corn fritters, fried bananas and bacon rolls.

COOK'S TIPS

Corn Fritters
Make up a batter from 125g (4oz) plain flour, a pinch of salt, 1 medium egg and 150ml (¼ pint) milk. Fold in 300g (11oz) drained or thawed sweetcorn kernels. Fry spoonfuls in a little hot fat until crisp and golden, turning them once. Drain well on kitchen paper.

Fried Bananas
Peel and slice 4 bananas lengthways and fry gently for about 3 minutes in a little hot butter until lightly browned.

Bacon Rolls
Roll up rashers of streaky bacon, rind removed, then thread on to a metal skewer and grill for about 3–5 minutes until crisp.

Fried Chicken

Preparation Time 5 minutes • Cooking Time 35–45 minutes • Serves 4 • Per Serving 565 calories, 42g fat (of which 10g saturates), 9g carbohydrate, 0.5g salt • Easy

4 chicken joints or pieces
3 tbsp plain flour
50g (2oz) butter or 3 tbsp
   vegetable oil
salt and ground black pepper
green salad to serve

1. Wipe the chicken joints and pat dry with kitchen paper. Season with salt and pepper.

2. Toss the chicken in the flour until completely coated.

3. Heat the butter or oil in a large frying pan or flameproof casserole over a high heat. Add the chicken and cook until golden brown on both sides. Reduce the heat and cook for 30–40 minutes until tender. Drain on kitchen paper. Serve with a green salad.

COOK'S TIP
To ensure that the chicken pieces remain moist, the surface should be browned at a high temperature to seal in all the juices and give a good colour; the heat should then be reduced for the remaining cooking time.

One-pan Chicken with Tomatoes

Preparation Time 5 minutes • Cooking Time 20–25 minutes • Serves 4 • Per Serving 238 calories, 4g fat (of which 1g saturates), 20g carbohydrate, 1g salt • Gluten Free • Dairy Free

4 chicken thighs

1 red onion, sliced

400g can chopped tomatoes with herbs

400g can mixed beans, drained and rinsed

2 tsp balsamic vinegar

freshly chopped flat-leafed parsley to garnish

1. Heat a non-stick pan and fry the chicken thighs, skin side down, for about 5 minutes or until golden. Turn over and fry the other side for 5 minutes.

2. Add the onion and fry for about 5 minutes. Add the tomatoes, mixed beans and vinegar, then cover and simmer for 10–12 minutes or until piping hot. Garnish with parsley and serve immediately.

TRY SOMETHING DIFFERENT
Use flageolet beans or other canned beans instead of mixed beans, and garnish with fresh basil or oregano.

Chicken with Wine & Capers

Preparation Time 5 minutes • Cooking Time 25 minutes • Serves 4 • Per Serving 234 calories, 10g fat (of which 5g saturates), trace carbohydrate, 0.3g salt • Gluten Free • Easy

1 tbsp olive oil
15g (½ oz) butter
4 small skinless chicken breasts
lemon wedges to garnish
rice to serve

FOR THE WINE AND CAPER SAUCE
125ml (4fl oz) white wine
3 tbsp capers, rinsed and drained
juice of 1 lemon
15g (½oz) butter
1 tbsp freshly chopped flat-leafed parsley

1. Heat the oil and butter in a large frying pan over a medium heat. Add the chicken breasts and fry for about 10–12 minutes on each side until cooked through. Transfer to a warmed plate, then cover and keep warm.

2. To make the sauce, add the wine and capers to the same pan. Bring to the boil, then reduce the heat and simmer for 2–3 minutes until the wine is reduced by half. Add the lemon juice and butter and stir in the parsley.

3. Divide the chicken among four warmed plates, pour the sauce over the chicken, garnish each serving with a lemon wedge and serve immediately with boiled rice.

Grilled Spicy Chicken

Preparation Time 10 minutes, plus marinating • Cooking Time about 20 minutes • Serves 4 •
Per Serving 157 calories, 2g fat (of which 1g saturates), 3g carbohydrate, 0.2g salt • Gluten Free • Easy

**4 boneless, skinless chicken
  breasts**
1 tbsp coriander seeds, crushed
1 tsp ground cumin
2 tsp mild curry paste
1 garlic clove, crushed
450g (1lb) natural yogurt
3 tbsp freshly chopped coriander
salt and ground black pepper
fresh coriander sprigs to garnish
mixed salad and rice to serve

1. Prick the chicken breasts all over with a fork, cover with clingfilm and lightly beat with a rolling pin to flatten them slightly.

2. Mix the coriander seeds with the cumin, curry paste, garlic and yogurt in a large shallow dish. Season with salt and pepper and stir in the chopped coriander.

3. Add the chicken and turn to coat with the spiced yogurt. Cover and leave to marinate in the fridge for at least 30 minutes or overnight.

4. Preheat the barbecue or griddle. Lift the chicken out of the marinade and cook over a medium-high heat, turning occasionally, for about 20 minutes or until cooked through. Serve immediately, with a mixed salad and rice, garnished with coriander sprigs.

Marinated Poussins

Preparation Time 30 minutes, plus marinating and soaking • Cooking Time 30 minutes • Serves 4 •
Per Serving 508 calories, 30g fat (of which 8g saturates), 10g carbohydrate, 1.6g salt • Gluten Free • Dairy Free • Easy

150ml (¼ pint) bourbon
15g (½oz) soft brown sugar
50ml (2fl oz) clear honey
50ml (2fl oz) tomato ketchup
2 tbsp wholegrain mustard
1 tbsp white wine vinegar
3 garlic cloves, crushed
**1 tsp each salt and ground black
    pepper**
4 poussins
**chargrilled peppers, tomatoes and
    onions, garnished with flat-
    leafed parsley, to serve**

1. Mix the bourbon, sugar, honey, tomato ketchup and mustard together. Stir in the vinegar, garlic, salt and pepper.

2. Put the poussins, breast side down, on a chopping board, then cut through either side of the backbone with poultry shears or a pair of strong sharp scissors and remove it. Open out the poussins, cover them with clingfilm and flatten them slightly by tapping them with the base of a pan. Put the poussins in a shallow glass dish and pour the bourbon marinade over the top, then cover, chill and leave to marinate overnight.

3. Preheat the barbecue or grill. Soak eight wooden skewers in water for 20 minutes. Thread the skewers through the legs and breasts of the poussins, keeping the marinade to one side. Cook the poussins for 30 minutes or until cooked through, basting from time to time with the reserved marinade. Serve with the peppers, tomatoes and onions garnished with the parsley.

**TRY SOMETHING
DIFFERENT**
*Use chicken joints instead of the
poussins, if you like.*

Spiced Chicken with Garlic Butter Beans

Preparation Time 10 minutes • Cooking Time 15 minutes • Serves 4 • Per Serving 443 calories, 16g fat (of which 3g saturates), 42g carbohydrate, 2g salt • Dairy Free • Easy

4 boneless, skinless chicken
    breasts, about 100g (3½oz) each
1 tbsp olive oil
1 tsp ground coriander
1 tsp ground cumin
100g (3½oz) couscous
3 tbsp extra virgin olive oil
1 garlic clove, sliced
2 × 400g cans butter beans, drained
    and rinsed
juice of 1 lemon
1 small red onion, thinly sliced
50g (2oz) marinated roasted
    peppers, drained
2 medium tomatoes, seeded and
    chopped
1 tbsp freshly chopped coriander
1 tbsp freshly chopped flat-leafed
    parsley
salt and ground black pepper
green salad and lemon wedges
    to serve

1. Put the chicken on a board, cover with clingfilm and flatten lightly with a rolling pin. Put the olive oil into a large bowl with the ground coriander and cumin. Mix together, then add the chicken and turn to coat.

2. Heat a large frying pan and cook the chicken for 5–7 minutes on each side until golden and the juices run clear when pierced with a skewer.

3. While the chicken is cooking, put the couscous into a bowl and add 100ml (3½fl oz) boiling water. Cover with clingfilm and set aside.

4. Put the extra virgin olive oil into a small pan with the garlic and butter beans and warm through for about 3–4 minutes over a low heat. Stir in the lemon juice and season with salt and pepper.

5. Fluff up the couscous with a fork and tip in the warm butter beans. Add the onion, peppers, tomatoes and herbs and stir together. Slice each chicken breast into four pieces and arrange alongside the bean salad. Serve with a green salad and lemon wedges to squeeze over.

Peas & Bacon with Pan-fried Chicken

Preparation Time 5 minutes • Cooking Time 20 minutes • Serves 4 • Per Serving 314 calories, 21g fat (of which 5g saturates), 7g carbohydrate, 0.9g salt • Gluten Free • Easy

4 skinless chicken breasts, about 125g (4oz) each
2 tbsp olive oil
2 shallots, finely sliced
3 unsmoked, rindless streaky bacon rashers, chopped
200g (7oz) frozen peas, thawed
2 tbsp sunblush tomato pesto
salt and ground black pepper
buttered new potatoes to serve

1. Preheat a griddle. Season the chicken generously with salt and pepper, then brush with 1 tbsp oil and cook on the griddle, skin side down, for 8–10 minutes. Turn over and continue to cook on the other side for 8–10 minutes until cooked through and the juices run clear when the chicken is pierced with a skewer.

2. Meanwhile, heat the remaining oil in a frying pan. Add the shallots and bacon and fry together until the shallots are softened and the bacon is golden. Add the peas and cook for 2 minutes, then stir in the pesto.

3. Serve the peas and bacon with the chicken breasts and new potatoes.

Lemon Chicken

Preparation Time 2 minutes • Cooking Time 6–8 minutes • Serves 4 • Per Serving 231 calories,
7g fat (of which 1g saturates), 13g carbohydrate, 0.2g salt • Gluten Free • Dairy Free • Easy

**4 small skinless chicken breasts,
about 125g (4oz) each**
juice of 2 lemons
2 tbsp olive oil
4–6 tbsp demerara sugar
salt
**green salad and lemon wedges
to serve**

1. Put the chicken into a large bowl and season with salt. Add the lemon juice and oil and stir to mix.

2. Preheat the grill to medium. Spread the chicken out on a large baking sheet and sprinkle over 2–3 tbsp demerara sugar. Grill for about 3–4 minutes or until caramelised, then turn the chicken over, sprinkle with the remaining sugar and grill until the chicken is golden and cooked through.

3. Divide the chicken among four plates and serve with a green salad and lemon wedges.

Chicken with Peanut Sauce

Preparation Time 10 minutes, plus marinating • Cooking Time about 10 minutes • Serves 4 • Per Serving 408 calories, 20g fat (of which 3g saturates), 19g carbohydrate, 0.5g salt • Gluten Free • Dairy Free • Easy

4 boneless, skinless chicken breasts, cut into strips
1 tbsp ground coriander
2 garlic cloves, finely chopped
4 tbsp vegetable oil
2 tbsp clear honey
fresh coriander sprigs to garnish
Thai rice to serve (see Cook's Tip)

FOR THE PEANUT SAUCE
1 tbsp vegetable oil
2 tbsp curry paste
2 tbsp brown sugar
2 tbsp peanut butter
200ml (7fl oz) coconut milk

1. Mix the chicken with the ground coriander, garlic, oil and honey. Cover, chill and leave to marinate for 15 minutes.

2. To make the peanut sauce, heat the oil in a pan. Add the curry paste, sugar and peanut butter and fry for 1 minute. Add the coconut milk and bring to the boil, stirring all the time, then reduce the heat and simmer for 5 minutes.

3. Meanwhile, heat a wok or large frying pan and, when hot, stir-fry the chicken and its marinade in batches for 3–4 minutes or until cooked, adding more oil if needed.

4. Serve the chicken on a bed of Thai rice, with the peanut sauce poured over. Garnish with coriander sprigs.

COOK'S TIP
Thai Rice
To serve six, you will need:
- *500g (1lb 2oz) Thai rice*
- *a handful of mint leaves*
- *salt*

Cook the rice and mint in lightly salted boiling water for about 10–12 minutes until tender. Drain well and serve.

TRY SOMETHING DIFFERENT
Replace the chicken with pork escalopes or rump steak, cut into thin strips.

Chicken Stir-fry with Noodles

Preparation Time 20 minutes • Cooking Time 20 minutes • Serves 4 • Per Serving 355 calories,
10g fat (of which 2g saturates), 29g carbohydrate, 0.5g salt • Dairy Free • Easy

250g pack thick egg noodles

2 tbsp vegetable oil

2 garlic cloves, crushed

**4 boneless, skinless chicken
breasts, each sliced into
10 pieces**

**3 medium carrots, about 450g (1lb),
cut into thin strips, about 5cm
(2in) long**

1 bunch of spring onions, sliced

200g (7oz) mangetouts

**155g jar sweet chilli and
lemongrass sauce**

1. Cook the noodles in boiling water according to the pack instructions.

2. Meanwhile, heat the oil in a wok or frying pan. Add the garlic and stir-fry for 1–2 minutes. Add the chicken and stir-fry for 5 minutes, then add the carrot strips and stir-fry for a further 5 minutes.

3. Add the spring onions, mangetouts and sauce to the wok and stir-fry for 5 minutes.

4. Drain the cooked noodles well and add to the wok. Toss everything together and serve.

**TRY SOMETHING
DIFFERENT**

*Use turkey or pork escalopes
instead of the chicken: you will
need 450g (1lb), cut into thin strips.*

Chicken with Oyster Sauce

Preparation Time 10 minutes • Cooking Time about 18 minutes • Serves 4 • Per Serving 344 calories,
23g fat (of which 3g saturates), 7g carbohydrate, 1.1g salt • Dairy Free • Easy

6 tbsp vegetable oil

**450g (1lb) boneless, skinless
chicken breasts, cut into
bite-size pieces**

3 tbsp oyster sauce

1 tbsp dark soy sauce

**100ml (3½fl oz) chicken stock
(see page 222)**

2 tsp lemon juice

1 garlic clove, thinly sliced

**6–8 large flat mushrooms, about
250g (9oz) total weight, sliced**

125g (4oz) mangetouts

**1 tsp cornflour mixed with 1 tbsp
water**

1 tbsp toasted sesame oil

salt and ground black pepper

rice to serve

1. Heat 3 tbsp vegetable oil in
a wok or large frying pan. Add
the chicken and cook over a high
heat, stirring continuously for
2–3 minutes until lightly browned.
Remove the chicken with a slotted
spoon and drain on kitchen paper.

2. Mix the oyster sauce with the
soy sauce, stock and lemon juice.
Add the chicken and mix
thoroughly.

3. Heat the remaining vegetable oil
in the pan over a high heat and stir-
fry the garlic for about 30 seconds.
Add the mushrooms and cook for
1 minute. Add the chicken mixture,
cover and simmer for 8 minutes.

4. Stir in the mangetouts and cook
for a further 2–3 minutes. Remove
the pan from the heat and stir in
the cornflour mixture. Put the pan
back on the heat, add the sesame
oil and stir until the sauce has
thickened. Season with salt and
pepper and serve immediately
with rice.

Quick Chicken Stir-fry

Preparation Time 10 minutes • Cooking Time 12 minutes • Serves 4 • Per Serving 316 calories,
3g fat (of which 1g saturates), 46g carbohydrate, 0.5g salt • Gluten Free • Dairy Free • Easy

1 tsp groundnut oil
300g (11oz) boneless, skinless
  chicken breasts, sliced
4 spring onions, chopped
200g (7oz) medium rice noodles
100g (3½oz) mangetouts
200g (7oz) purple sprouting
  broccoli, chopped
2–3 tbsp sweet chilli sauce
coriander leaves to garnish
lime wedges (optional) to serve

1. Heat the oil in a wok or large frying pan. Add the chicken and spring onions and stir-fry over a high heat for 5–6 minutes until the chicken is golden.

2. Meanwhile, soak the rice noodles in boiling water for 4 minutes or according to the pack instructions.

3. Add the mangetouts, broccoli and chilli sauce to the chicken. Continue to stir-fry for 4 minutes.

4. Drain the noodles, then add to the pan and toss everything together. Scatter the coriander leaves over the top and serve with lime wedges to squeeze over the stir-fry, if you like.

**TRY SOMETHING
DIFFERENT**
Other vegetables are just as good in this dish: try pak choi, button mushrooms, carrots cut into matchsticks, or baby sweetcorn.

Chicken with Vegetables & Noodles

Preparation Time 10 minutes • Cooking Time about 12 minutes • Serves 2 • Per Serving 584 calories, 19g fat (of which 3g saturates), 67g carbohydrate, 4.1g salt • Dairy Free • Easy

225g (8oz) fine egg noodles

about 2 tbsp vegetable oil

1 large boneless, skinless chicken breast, about 150g (5oz), cut into very thin strips

2.5cm (1in) piece fresh root ginger, peeled and finely chopped

1 garlic clove, finely chopped

1 red pepper, seeded and thinly sliced

4 spring onions, thinly sliced

2 carrots, thinly sliced

125g (4oz) shiitake or button mushrooms, halved

a handful of bean sprouts (optional)

3 tbsp hoisin sauce

2 tbsp light soy sauce

1 tbsp chilli sauce

shredded spring onion and sesame seeds to garnish

1. Bring a large pan of water to the boil and cook the noodles for about 3 minutes or according to the pack instructions. Drain thoroughly and toss with a little of the oil to prevent them sticking together. Set aside.

2. Heat the remaining oil in a wok or large frying pan. Add the chicken, ginger and garlic and stir-fry over a very high heat for about 5 minutes or until the chicken is browned on the outside and cooked right through.

3. Add all the vegetables to the pan and stir-fry over a high heat for about 2 minutes or until they are just cooked, but still crunchy.

4. Stir in the hoisin, soy and chilli sauces and mix well. Add the noodles, toss well to mix and cook for a couple of minutes until heated through. Serve immediately sprinkled with shredded spring onion and sesame seeds.

TRY SOMETHING DIFFERENT
* *Replace the chicken with thinly sliced turkey escalopes.*
* *Increase the heat of the dish by frying a chopped chilli with the garlic and ginger.*

Mild Spiced Chicken & Quinoa

Preparation Time 15 minutes • Cooking Time 20 minutes • Serves 4 • Per Serving 268 calories,
3g fat (of which trace saturates), 37g carbohydrate, 0.4g salt • Gluten Free • Dairy Free • Easy

2 tbsp Mango Chutney
   (see page 44)
juice of ½ lemon
1 tbsp olive oil
2 tsp mild curry powder
1 tsp paprika
350g (12oz) skinless chicken
   breast, cut into thick strips
200g (7oz) quinoa (see Cook's Tip)

1 cucumber, roughly chopped
½ bunch of spring onions, sliced
75g (3oz) ready-to-eat dried
   apricots, sliced
2 tbsp freshly chopped mint, basil
   or tarragon
salt and ground black pepper
fresh mint sprigs to garnish

1. Put the chutney, lemon juice, ½ tbsp oil, the curry powder, paprika and salt and pepper into a bowl and mix together. Add the chicken strips and toss to coat.

2. Cook the quinoa in boiling water for 10–12 minutes until tender or according to the pack instructions. Drain thoroughly. Put into a bowl, then stir in the cucumber, spring onions, apricots, herbs and remaining oil.

3. Put the chicken and marinade into a pan and fry over a high heat for 2–3 minutes, then add 150ml (¼ pint) water. Bring to the boil, then reduce the heat and simmer for 5 minutes or until the chicken is cooked through. Serve with the quinoa garnished with mint.

COOK'S TIP
Quinoa is a tiny, bead-shaped grain with a slightly nutty flavour. It's easy to prepare and nearly quadruples in size and looks translucent when cooked. It can be substituted for rice or couscous.

Chicken & Basil Pasta

Preparation Time 5 minutes • Cooking Time 15 minutes • Serves 4 • Per Serving 415 calories,
9g fat (of which 2g saturates), 62g carbohydrate, 0.9g salt • Dairy Free • Easy

300g (11oz) pasta
1 tbsp olive oil
1 garlic clove, crushed
2 × 400g cans cherry tomatoes
300g (11oz) cooked chicken,
shredded
50g (2oz) pitted black olives
a handful of torn basil leaves
salt and ground black pepper
green salad to serve (optional)

1. Cook the pasta in a large pan of lightly salted boiling water or according to the pack instructions.

2. Meanwhile, heat the oil in a pan. Add the garlic and cook for about 1–2 minutes, then add the tomatoes and cook for a further 5–7 minutes.

3. Add the shredded chicken and black olives to the pan and cook for 2–3 minutes. Stir in the basil and season with salt and pepper.

4. Drain the pasta, toss in the sauce and serve immediately with a green salad, if you like.

Pasta with Chicken, Cream & Basil

Preparation Time 10 minutes • Cooking Time 25 minutes • Serves 4 • Per Serving 612 calories,
27g fat (of which 12g saturates), 67g carbohydrate, 0.4g salt • Easy

1 tbsp olive oil

2 shallots, chopped

400g (14oz) boneless chicken,
  cubed

125g (4oz) chestnut mushrooms,
  sliced

50g (2oz) sultanas

a pinch of ground cinnamon

50ml (2fl oz) dry white wine

125ml (4fl oz) hot chicken stock
  (see page 222)

300g (11oz) farfalle pasta

142ml carton double cream

2 tsp Dijon mustard

2 tsp freshly chopped basil

salt

1. Heat the oil in a pan. Add the shallots and fry for 4–5 minutes. Add the chicken and cook until browned. Add the mushrooms and cook for 2 minutes. Stir in the sultanas and cinnamon.

2. Pour in the wine and hot stock and simmer for 12–15 minutes until the chicken is cooked.

3. Meanwhile, cook the pasta in a large pan of lightly salted boiling water according to the pack instructions.

4. Stir the cream, mustard and basil into the chicken and season with salt. Drain the pasta and return to the pan, then add the sauce, toss and serve.

Chicken, Bacon & Leek Pasta Bake

Preparation Time 10 minutes • Cooking Time about 20 minutes • Serves 4 • Per Serving 650 calories, 24g fat (of which 6g saturates), 68g carbohydrate, 2.2g salt • Easy

1 tbsp olive oil

100g (3½oz) bacon lardons

450g (1lb) boneless, skinless chicken thighs, chopped

3 medium leeks, trimmed and chopped

300g (11oz) macaroni or other pasta shapes

350g carton ready-made cheese sauce

2 tsp Dijon mustard

25g (1oz) freshly grated Parmesan

salt

2 tbsp freshly chopped flat-leafed parsley to garnish

1. Heat the oil in a large frying pan. Add the bacon and chicken and cook for 7–8 minutes. Add the leeks and continue cooking for 4–5 minutes.

2. Meanwhile, cook the pasta in a large pan of lightly salted boiling water according to the pack instructions. Drain well.

3. Preheat the grill. Add the cheese sauce to the pasta with the mustard and chicken mixture. Mix well, then tip into a 2.1 litre (3¾ pint) ovenproof dish and sprinkle with Parmesan. Grill for 4–5 minutes until golden, then garnish with chopped parsley.

CASSEROLES, STEWS & BRAISES

Classic Coq au Vin

Preparation Time 15 minutes • Cooking Time 2 hours • Serves 6 • Per Serving 740 calories, 44.3g fat (of which 17.1g saturates), 25.9g carbohydrate, 1.8g salt • A Little Effort

1 large chicken jointed (see page 223) or 6–8 chicken joints
2 tbsp well-seasoned flour
100g (3½oz) butter
125g (4oz) lean bacon, diced
1 medium onion, quartered
1 medium carrot, quartered
4 tbsp brandy
600ml (1 pint) red wine
1 garlic clove, crushed
1 bouquet garni (see Cook's Tip, page 26)
1 sugar lump
2 tbsp vegetable oil
450g (1lb) button onions
a pinch of sugar
1 tsp wine vinegar
225g (8oz) button mushrooms
6 slices white bread, crusts removed
salt and ground black pepper

1. Coat the chicken pieces with 1 tbsp seasoned flour. Melt 25g (1oz) butter in a flameproof casserole. Add the chicken and fry gently until golden brown on all sides. Add the bacon, onion and carrot and fry until softened.

2. Heat the brandy in a small pan, pour over the chicken and ignite, shaking the pan so that all the chicken pieces are covered in flames. Pour in the wine and stir to dislodge any sediment from the base of the casserole. Add the garlic, bouquet garni and sugar lump and bring to the boil. Reduce the heat, cover and simmer for 1–1½ hours or until the chicken is cooked through.

3. Meanwhile, melt 25g (1oz) butter with 1 tsp oil in a frying pan. Add the button onions and fry until they begin to brown. Add the pinch of sugar and vinegar together with 1 tbsp water. Cover and simmer for 10–15 minutes until just tender. Keep warm.

4. Melt 25g (1oz) butter with 2 tsp oil in a pan. Add the mushrooms and cook for a few minutes, then turn off the heat and keep warm.

5. Remove the chicken from the casserole and place in a dish. Surround with the onions and mushrooms and keep hot.

6. Discard the bouquet garni. Skim the excess fat from the cooking liquid, then boil the liquid in the casserole briskly for 3–5 minutes to reduce it.

7. Add the remaining oil to the fat in the frying pan and fry the pieces of bread until golden brown on both sides. Cut each slice into triangles.

8. Work the remaining butter and flour to make a beurre manié (see page 102). Remove the casserole from the heat and add small pieces of the beurre manié to the cooking liquid. Stir until smooth, then put back on to the heat and bring just to the boil. The sauce should be thick and shiny. Take off the heat and adjust the seasoning. Return the chicken, onions and mushrooms to the casserole and stir to combine. Garnish with the fried bread and serve.

Chicken with Chorizo & Beans

Preparation Time 10 minutes • Cooking Time 1 hour 5 minutes–1 hour 10 minutes • Serves 6 •
Per Serving 690 calories, 41g fat (of which 12g saturates), 33g carbohydrate, 2.6g salt • Dairy Free • Easy

1 tbsp olive oil
12 chicken pieces (6 drumsticks and 6 thighs)
175g (6oz) chorizo sausage, cubed
1 onion, finely chopped
2 large garlic cloves, crushed
1 tsp mild chilli powder
3 red peppers, seeded and roughly chopped
400g (14oz) passata

2 tbsp tomato purée
300ml (½ pint) hot chicken stock (see page 222)
2 × 400g cans butter beans, drained and rinsed
200g (7oz) new potatoes, halved
1 small bunch of thyme
1 bay leaf
200g (7oz) baby leaf spinach

1. Preheat the oven to 190°C (170°C fan oven) mark 5. Heat the oil in a large flameproof casserole and brown the chicken all over. Remove from the pan and set aside. Add the chorizo to the casserole and fry for 2–3 minutes until its oil starts to run. Add the onion, garlic and chilli powder and fry over a low heat for 5 minutes or until soft.

2. Add the peppers and cook for 2–3 minutes until soft. Stir in the passata, tomato purée, stock, butter beans, potatoes, thyme sprigs and bay leaf. Cover and simmer for 10 minutes.

3. Return the chicken and any juices to the casserole. Bring to a simmer, then cover and cook in the oven for 30–35 minutes. If the sauce looks thin, return the casserole to the hob over a medium heat and simmer to reduce until nicely thick.

4. Remove the thyme and bay leaf, then stir in the spinach until it wilts. Serve immediately.

TRY SOMETHING DIFFERENT
Use mixed beans instead of the butter beans.

One-pot Chicken

Preparation Time 20 minutes • Cooking Time 1 hour 40 minutes • Serves 6 • Per Serving 474 calories, 33g fat (of which 9g saturates), 6g carbohydrate, 0.6g salt • Dairy Free • Easy

2 tbsp olive oil
1 large onion, cut into wedges
2 rindless streaky bacon rashers, chopped
1 chicken, about 1.6kg (3½lb)
6 carrots
2 small turnips, cut into wedges
1 garlic clove, crushed
bouquet garni (1 bay leaf, a few fresh parsley and thyme sprigs)

600ml (1 pint) hot chicken stock (see page 222)
100ml (3½fl oz) dry white wine
12 button mushrooms
3 tbsp freshly chopped flat-leafed parsley
salt and ground black pepper
mashed potatoes to serve (optional)

1. Heat the oil in a non-stick flameproof casserole. Add the onion and bacon and fry for 5 minutes or until golden. Remove and put to one side.

2. Add the whole chicken to the casserole and fry for 10 minutes, turning carefully to brown all over. Remove and put to one side.

3. Preheat the oven to 200°C (180°C fan oven) mark 6. Add the carrots, turnips and garlic to the casserole and fry for 5 minutes, then add the onion and bacon. Put the chicken back into the casserole, add the bouquet garni, hot stock and wine and season with salt and pepper. Bring to a simmer, then cover the pan and cook in the oven for 30 minutes.

4. Remove the casserole from the oven and add the mushrooms. Baste the chicken, then re-cover and cook for a further 50 minutes.

5. Lift out the chicken, then stir the parsley into the cooking liquid. Carve the chicken and serve with the vegetables and cooking liquid, and mashed potatoes, if you like.

TRY SOMETHING DIFFERENT
Use chicken pieces such as drumsticks or thighs, reducing the cooking time in step 4 to 20 minutes.

Chicken in Red Wine

Preparation Time 15 minutes • Cooking Time 1 hour 10 minutes • Serves 4 • Per Serving 358 calories, 14g fat (of which 4g saturates), 8g carbohydrate, 1.1g salt • Dairy Free • Easy

8 slices prosciutto
8 large boneless, skinless chicken thighs
1 tbsp olive oil
1 fat garlic clove, crushed
about 12 shallots or button onions
225g (8oz) fresh shiitake mushrooms
1 tbsp plain flour
300ml (½ pint) red wine
300ml (½ pint) hot chicken stock (see page 222)
1 tbsp Worcestershire sauce
1 bay leaf
salt and ground black pepper
crusty bread to serve

1. Wrap a slice of prosciutto around each chicken thigh. Heat the oil in a large non-stick frying pan and fry the chicken thighs in batches for 8–10 minutes until golden brown all over. Transfer to a plate and put to one side.

2. Add the garlic and shallots or button onions and fry over a low heat for 5 minutes or until the shallots are beginning to soften and turn golden. Stir in the mushrooms and flour and cook over a low heat for 1–2 minutes.

3. Put the chicken back in the pan and add the wine, hot stock, Worcestershire sauce and bay leaf. Season lightly with salt and pepper, bring to the boil for 5 minutes, then reduce the heat to low, cover and simmer for 45 minutes or until the chicken is cooked through and the juices run clear when the thickest part of the thigh is pierced with a skewer. Serve with crusty bread.

COOK'S TIPS

• *If you can't buy prosciutto, thinly cut smoked streaky bacon will work just as well.*
• *Use button mushrooms if you can't find shiitake.*

FREEZING TIP

To freeze This dish is ideal for freezing for an easy meal another day. Double the quantities and make another meal for four or make two meals for two people and freeze. Complete the recipe, cool quickly, then put into a freezerproof container and freeze for up to three months.
To use Thaw overnight at cool room temperature, then put back into a large pan. Bring slowly to the boil, then reduce the heat and simmer gently for about 10–15 minutes until piping hot.

Chicken in White Wine Sauce

Preparation Time 45 minutes • Cooking Time about 1 hour • Serves 4 • Per Serving 787 calories,
51g fat (of which 22g saturates), 24g carbohydrate, 1.5g salt • A Little Effort

**750ml bottle full-bodied white wine,
  such as Chardonnay**

4 tbsp brandy

**2 bouquet garni (see Cook's Tip,
  page 26)**

1 garlic clove, bruised

plain flour to coat

**1 chicken, about 1.4kg (3lb), jointed
  (see page 223), or 2 boneless
  breasts, halved, plus
  2 drumsticks and 2 thighs**

125g (4oz) butter

**125g (4oz) rindless unsmoked bacon
  rashers, cut into strips**

**225g (8oz) baby onions, peeled with
  root ends intact**

**225g (8oz) brown-cap mushrooms,
  halved, or quartered if large**

**25g (1oz) butter mixed with 25g
  (1oz) plain flour (beurre manié,
  see Cook's Tip, page 102)**

salt and ground black pepper

buttered noodles or rice to serve

1. Preheat the oven to 180°C
(160°C fan oven) mark 4. Pour the
wine and brandy into a pan. Add
1 bouquet garni and the garlic.
Bring to the boil, then reduce the
heat and simmer until reduced by
half. Cool.

2. Season the flour with salt and
pepper and use to coat the chicken
joints lightly. Melt half the butter in a
large frying pan. When foaming, add
the chicken joints and brown all over
(in batches if necessary). Transfer
to a flameproof casserole. Add the
bacon to the frying pan and fry until
golden. Remove with a slotted spoon
and add to the chicken.

3. Strain the cooled reduced wine
mixture over the chicken and add
the other bouquet garni. Bring to
the boil, cover and cook in the oven
for 30 minutes.

4. Meanwhile, melt the remaining
butter in a frying pan and fry the
onions until tender and lightly
browned. Add the mushrooms
and fry until softened.

5. Add the mushrooms and onions
to the casserole, cover and cook
for a further 10 minutes or until
the chicken is tender. Lift out the
chicken and vegetables with
a slotted spoon and put into a
warmed serving dish. Cover
and keep warm.

6. Bring the cooking liquid in the
casserole to the boil. Whisk in
the beurre manié, a piece at a time,
until the sauce is shiny and syrupy.
Check the seasoning.

7. Pour the sauce over the chicken.
Serve with buttered noodles or rice.

Chicken & Vegetable Hotpot

Preparation Time 5 minutes • Cooking Time 30 minutes • Serves 4 • Per Serving 338 calories, 14g fat (of which 3g saturates), 14g carbohydrate, 1.2g salt • Dairy Free • Easy

4 chicken breasts, with skin, about 125g (4oz) each
2 large parsnips, chopped
2 large carrots, chopped
300ml (½ pint) ready-made gravy
125g (4oz) cabbage, shredded
ground black pepper

1. Heat a non-stick frying pan or flameproof casserole until hot. Add the chicken breasts, skin side down, and cook for 5–6 minutes. Turn them over, add the parsnips and carrots and cook for a further 7–8 minutes.

2. Pour the gravy over the chicken and vegetables, then cover the pan and cook gently for 10 minutes.

3. Season with pepper and stir in the cabbage, then cover and continue to cook for 4–5 minutes until the chicken is cooked through, the cabbage has wilted and the vegetables are tender. Serve hot.

Slow-braised Garlic Chicken

Preparation Time 30 minutes • Cooking Time about 2 hours • Serves 6 • Per Serving 506 calories, 28g fat (of which 9g saturates), 10g carbohydrate, 1g salt • A Little Effort

2 tbsp olive oil

1 tbsp freshly chopped thyme

125g (4oz) chestnut mushrooms, finely chopped

6 whole chicken legs (drumsticks and thighs)

18 thin slices pancetta

2 tbsp plain flour

25g (1oz) butter

18 small shallots

12 garlic cloves, unpeeled but split

750ml bottle full-bodied white wine, such as Chardonnay

2 bay leaves

salt and ground black pepper

1. Preheat the oven to 180°C (160°C fan oven) mark 4. Heat 1 tbsp oil in a frying pan. Add the thyme and mushrooms and fry until the moisture has evaporated. Season with salt and pepper and cool.

2. Loosen the skin away from one chicken leg and spoon a little of the mushroom paste underneath. Season the leg all over with salt and pepper, then wrap three pancetta slices around the thigh end. Repeat with the remaining chicken legs, then dust using 1 tbsp flour.

3. Melt the butter in a frying pan with the remaining oil over a high heat. Fry the chicken legs, in batches, seam side down, until golden. Turn the legs, brown the other side, then transfer to a casserole. The browning should take 8–10 minutes per batch.

4. Put the shallots and garlic into the frying pan and cook for 10 minutes or until browned. Sprinkle over the remaining flour and cook for 1 minute. Pour in the wine and bring to the boil, stirring. Pour into the casserole with the chicken and add the bay leaves. Cover and cook in the oven for 1½ hours. Serve hot.

FREEZING TIP

To freeze *Complete the recipe to the end of step 4. Cool quickly, then freeze in an airtight container for up to one month.*

To use *Thaw overnight at cool room temperature. Preheat the oven to 220°C (200°C fan oven) mark 7. Put the chicken back into the casserole and reheat in the oven for 15 minutes. Reduce the oven temperature to 180°C (160°C fan oven) mark 4 and cook for a further 25 minutes.*

Easy Chicken Casserole

Preparation Time 15 minutes • Cooking Time 50 minutes • Serves 6 • Per Serving 323 calories,
18g fat (of which 5g saturates), 17g carbohydrate, 0.9g salt • Gluten Free • Dairy Free • Easy

1 fresh rosemary sprig

2 bay leaves

1.4kg (3lb) chicken

1 red onion, cut into wedges

2 carrots, cut into chunks

2 leeks, trimmed and cut into
   chunks

2 celery sticks, cut into chunks

12 baby new potatoes, halved
   if large

900ml (1½ pints) hot chicken stock
   (see page 222)

200g (7oz) green beans, trimmed

salt and ground black pepper

1. Preheat the oven to 180°C
(160°C fan oven) mark 4. Put the
herbs and chicken into a large,
flameproof casserole. Add the
onion, carrots, leeks, celery,
potatoes, stock and seasoning.
Bring to the boil, then cook in
the oven for 45 minutes or until the
chicken is cooked through. To test
the chicken, pierce the thickest
part of the leg with a knife; the
juices should run clear.

2. Add the beans and cook for
5 minutes. Remove the chicken
and spoon the vegetables into
six bowls. Carve the chicken and
divide among the bowls, the ladle
the cooking liquid over.

**TRY SOMETHING
DIFFERENT**
*Omit the baby new potatoes and
serve with mashed potatoes.*

DISHES FROM AROUND THE WORLD

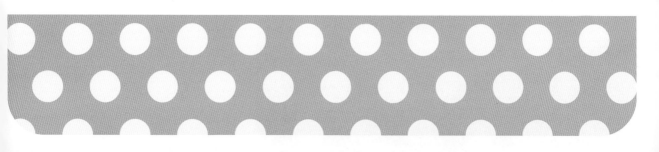

Alsace Chicken

Preparation Time 20 minutes • Cooking Time 1 hour 20 minutes • Serves 4 • Per Serving 484 calories, 24g fat (of which 8g saturates), 11g carbohydrate, 1.4g salt • Easy

2 tbsp vegetable oil
8 chicken pieces (such as breasts, thighs and drumsticks)
125g (4oz) rindless smoked streaky bacon rashers, cut into strips
12 shallots, peeled but left whole
3 fresh tarragon sprigs
1 tbsp plain flour

150ml (¼ pint) Alsace Riesling white wine
500ml (18fl oz) hot chicken stock (see page 222)
3 tbsp crème fraîche
salt and ground black pepper
new potatoes (optional) and green beans to serve

1. Heat half the oil in a frying pan over a medium heat. Fry the chicken, in batches, until golden, adding more oil to the pan as necessary. Set aside.

2. Put the bacon into the same pan and fry gently to release its fat. Add the shallots and cook for 5 minutes, stirring occasionally, or until both the shallots and bacon are lightly coloured.

3. Strip the leaves from the tarragon and put both the leaves and stalks to one side. Sprinkle the flour over the shallots and bacon and stir to absorb the juices. Cook for 1 minute, then gradually add the wine, hot stock and tarragon stalks. Put the chicken back into the pan, cover and simmer over a gentle heat for 45 minutes–1 hour until the chicken is cooked through.

4. Remove the chicken, bacon and shallots with a slotted spoon and keep warm. Discard the tarragon stalks. Bubble the sauce until reduced by half. Stir in the crème fraîche and tarragon leaves. Season with salt and pepper.

5. Turn off the heat, put the chicken, bacon and shallots back into the pan and stir to combine. Serve with new potatoes and green beans.

Chicken & Mushroom Stroganoff

Preparation Time 20 minutes • Cooking Time 30 minutes • Serves 4 • Per Serving 494 calories,
43g fat (of which 17g saturates), 4g carbohydrate, 0.3g salt • Easy

2 tbsp olive oil
1 onion, roughly chopped
2 garlic cloves, crushed
4 × 125g (4oz) chicken thighs,
    including skin and bones
250g (9oz) closed-cup mushrooms,
    roughly chopped
200g (7oz) brown rice, rinsed

175ml (6fl oz) hot chicken stock
    (see page 222)
150ml (¼ pint) double cream
leaves from 2 thyme sprigs, plus
    extra to garnish (optional)
50g (2oz) baby leaf spinach
salt and ground black pepper

1. Heat 1 tbsp oil in a pan. Add the onion and garlic, cover and cook gently for 10–15 minutes until soft. Remove from the pan and put to one side. Increase the heat to medium and add the remaining oil. Fry the chicken until golden. Add the mushrooms and cook for 5 minutes or until most of the liquid has evaporated.

2. Put the rice into a separate pan, then pour in 450ml (¾ pint) hot water. Cover and bring to the boil, then reduce the heat and cook according to the pack instructions.

3. Return the onion mixture to the chicken pan and gradually stir in the hot stock. Use a wooden spoon to scrape all the goodness from the base of the pan, then stir in the cream and thyme leaves. Simmer for 5 minutes.

4. Remove the chicken, discard the skin and bones and pull the meat into pieces. Return it to the pan. Add the spinach and stir to wilt. Taste for seasoning.

5. To serve, divide the rice among four warmed plates and ladle the stroganoff over the top. Garnish with thyme leaves, if you like.

Chicken Tabbouleh with Tomato Dressing

Preparation Time 50 minutes, plus marinating and soaking • Cooking Time 45 minutes • Serves 4 •
Per Serving 777 calories, 33g fat (of which 6g saturates), 50g carbohydrate, 0.6g salt • Dairy Free • Easy

1 large red chilli, seeded and finely chopped (see Cook's Tips, page 8)
3 garlic cloves, crushed
juice of 4 limes: about 8 tbsp juice
½ tsp ground turmeric
4 chicken breast quarters (breast and wing), about 300g (11oz) each, lightly scored
450g (1lb) tomatoes, preferably plum, chopped
2 tbsp capers
1 tbsp sugar
225g (8oz) bulgur wheat
125g (4oz) cucumber, chopped
50g (2oz) pinenuts, toasted
3 tbsp freshly chopped parsley
3 tbsp freshly chopped chives
50g (2oz) raisins
5 tbsp olive oil
225g (8oz) onions, thinly sliced
salt and ground black pepper
lime slices and fresh flat-leafed parsley to garnish (optional)

1. Put the chilli into a non-metallic bowl with the garlic, 3 tbsp lime juice and the turmeric. Add the chicken and stir well to coat. Cover the bowl, chill and leave to marinate for at least 3 hours.

2. Mix the tomatoes with the capers, 2 tbsp lime juice, the sugar and seasoning.

3. Put the bulgur wheat into a bowl, cover with 600ml (1 pint) boiling water and leave to soak for 30 minutes. Drain, then stir in the cucumber, pinenuts, herbs, raisins, remaining lime juice and 3 tbsp oil. Season with salt and pepper.

4. Preheat the oven to 240°C (220°C fan oven) mark 9. Drain the chicken, putting the marinade to one side. Put, skin side up, in a roasting tin with the remaining oil and onions. Cook in the oven for 30–35 minutes until done. Put to one side. Add the tomato mixture and remaining marinade to the roasting tin and put back in the oven for 5 minutes.

5. Spoon the dressing over the chicken. Garnish with lime slices and parsley, if you like, and serve at room temperature with the tabbouleh.

COOK'S TIP
Bulgur wheat is grains of wheat that have been boiled until they crack, and then dried. It is reconstituted in water.

Chicken Cacciatore

Preparation Time 5 minutes • Cooking Time 40 minutes • Serves 4 • Per Serving 327 calories,
17g fat (of which 4g saturates), 3g carbohydrate, 1.3g salt • Gluten Free • Dairy Free • Easy

2 tbsp olive oil
8 boneless, skinless chicken thighs
2 garlic cloves, crushed
1 tsp dried thyme
1 tsp dried tarragon
150ml (¼ pint) white wine
400g can chopped tomatoes
12 pitted black olives
12 capers, rinsed and drained
ground black pepper
brown rice and broad beans or peas
**   to serve**

1. Heat the oil in a flameproof casserole over a high heat. Add the chicken and brown all over. Reduce the heat and add the garlic, thyme, tarragon and wine to the casserole. Stir for 1 minute, then add the tomatoes and season with pepper.

2. Bring to the boil, then reduce the heat, cover the casserole and simmer for 20 minutes or until the chicken is tender.

3. Lift the chicken out of the casserole and put to one side. Bubble the sauce for 5 minutes or until thickened, add the olives and capers, stir well and cook for a further 2–3 minutes.

4. Put the chicken into the sauce. Serve with brown rice and broad beans or peas.

Spanish Chicken Parcels

Preparation Time 15 minutes • Cooking Time about 30 minutes • Serves 6 • Per Serving 444 calories,
29g fat (of which 9g saturates), 4g carbohydrate, 3.1g salt • Gluten Free • Dairy Free • Easy

12 boneless, skinless chicken thighs, about 900g (2lb)
180g jar pimientos or roasted red peppers, drained
12 thin slices chorizo sausage
2 tbsp olive oil
1 onion, finely chopped
4 garlic cloves, crushed
225g can chopped tomatoes
4 tbsp dry sherry
18 queen green olives (see Cook's Tip)
salt and ground black pepper
rice or crusty bread to serve

1. Put the chicken thighs on a board, season well with salt and pepper and put a piece of pimiento or roasted pepper inside each one. Wrap a slice of chorizo around the outside and secure with two cocktail sticks. Put to one side.

2. Heat the oil in a pan over a medium heat. Add the onion and fry for 10 minutes. Add the garlic and cook for 1 minute. Put the chicken parcels, chorizo side down, into the pan and brown them all over for 10–15 minutes.

3. Add the tomatoes and sherry to the pan and bring to the boil. Reduce the heat and simmer for 5 minutes or until the juices run clear when the chicken is pierced with a skewer. Add the olives and warm through. Remove the cocktail sticks and serve with rice or crusty bread.

COOK'S TIP
Queen green olives are large meaty olives with a mild flavour. Remember to tell people the olives still have stones.

Saffron Paella

Preparation Time 35 minutes • Cooking Time 50 minutes • Serves 6 • Per Serving 609 calories,
22g fat (of which 6g saturates), 59g carbohydrate, 1.5g salt • Dairy Free • Easy

½ tsp saffron threads

900ml–1.1 litres (1½–2 pints) hot
chicken stock (see page 222)

5 tbsp olive oil

2 × 70g packs sliced chorizo
sausage

6 boneless, skinless chicken
thighs, each cut into three pieces

1 large onion, chopped

4 large garlic cloves, crushed

1 tsp paprika

2 red peppers, seeded and sliced

400g can chopped tomatoes in
tomato juice

350g (12oz) long-grain rice

200ml (7fl oz) dry sherry

500g pack ready-cooked mussels

200g (7oz) cooked tiger prawns,
drained

juice of ½ lemon

salt and ground black pepper

fresh flat-leafed parsley sprigs to
garnish (optional)

lemon wedges to serve

1. Add the saffron to the hot stock and leave to infuse for 30 minutes. Meanwhile, heat half the oil in a large heavy-based frying pan. Add half the chorizo and fry for about 3–4 minutes or until crisp. Remove with a slotted spoon and drain on kitchen paper. Repeat with the remaining chorizo, then put the chorizo to one side.

2. Heat 1 tbsp oil in the pan. Add half the chicken and cook for 3–5 minutes until pale golden brown. Remove from the pan and put to one side. Cook the remaining chicken and put to one side.

3. Reduce the heat slightly, heat the remaining oil and add the onion. Cook for 5 minutes or until soft. Add the garlic and paprika and cook for 1 minute. Put the chicken back into the pan, then add the peppers and the tomatoes.

4. Stir the rice into the pan, then add one-third of the stock and bring to the boil. Season with salt and pepper, reduce the heat and simmer, uncovered, stirring continuously until most of the liquid has been absorbed.

5. Add the remaining stock, a little at a time, allowing the liquid to become absorbed after each addition (this should take about 25 minutes). Add the sherry and cook for a further 2 minutes.

6. Add the mussels and their juices to the pan with the prawns, lemon juice and reserved chorizo. Cook for 5 minutes to heat through. Adjust the seasoning and garnish with the parsley, if you like, and serve with lemon wedges.

Spiced Chicken Pilau

Preparation Time 15 minutes • Cooking Time 35–40 minutes • Serves 4 • Per Serving 649 calories, 18g fat (of which 2g saturates), 87g carbohydrate, 2.8g salt • Dairy Free • Easy

50g (2oz) pinenuts
2 tbsp olive oil
2 onions, sliced
2 garlic cloves, crushed
2 tbsp medium curry powder
6 boneless, skinless chicken thighs or 450g (1lb) skinless cooked chicken, cut into strips

350g (12oz) American easy-cook rice
2 tsp salt
a pinch of saffron threads
50g (2oz) sultanas
225g (8oz) ripe tomatoes, roughly chopped

1. Preheat the grill. Spread the pinenuts over a baking sheet and toast under the grill until golden brown, turning them frequently. Put to one side.

2. Heat the oil in a large heavy-based pan over a medium heat. Add the onions and garlic and cook for 5 minutes or until soft. Remove half the onion mixture from the pan and put to one side.

3. Add the curry powder and cook for 1 minute, then add the chicken and stir. Cook for 10 minutes if the meat is raw, or for 4 minutes if you're using cooked chicken, stirring from time to time until browned.

4. Add the rice to the pan and stir to coat in the oil, then add 900ml (1½ pints) boiling water, the salt and saffron. Cover the pan and bring to the boil, then reduce the heat to low and cook for 20 minutes or until the rice is tender and most of the liquid has been absorbed. Stir in the reserved onion mixture and the sultanas, tomatoes and pinenuts. Cook for a further 5 minutes to warm through, then serve.

COOK'S TIP
This is a good way to use leftover roast chicken or turkey.

Chicken Tagine with Apricots & Almonds

Preparation Time 10 minutes • Cooking Time about 1 hour • Serves 4 • Per Serving 376 calories, 22g fat (of which 4g saturates), 19g carbohydrate, 0.5g salt • Gluten Free • Dairy Free • Easy

2 tbsp olive oil
4 chicken thighs
1 onion, chopped
2 tsp ground cinnamon
2 tbsp runny honey
150g (5oz) ready-to-eat dried apricots

75g (3oz) blanched almonds
125ml (4fl oz) hot chicken stock (see page 222)
salt and ground black pepper
flaked almonds to garnish
couscous to serve

1. Heat 1 tbsp oil in a large pan over a medium heat. Add the chicken and fry for 5 minutes or until brown. Remove from the casserole and put to one side to keep warm.

2. Add the onion to the pan with the remaining oil and fry for 10 minutes or until softened.

3. Put the chicken back into the casserole with the cinnamon, honey, apricots, almonds and hot stock. Season well with salt and pepper, stir once, then cover and bring to the boil. Simmer for 45 minutes or until the chicken is falling off the bone.

4. Garnish with the flaked almonds and serve hot with couscous.

Moroccan Chicken with Chickpeas

Preparation Time 10 minutes • Cooking Time 50 minutes • Serves 6 • Per Serving 440 calories, 18g fat (of which 6g saturates), 33g carbohydrate, 1g salt • Easy

12 chicken pieces, including thighs, drumsticks and breasts
25g (1oz) butter
1 large onion, sliced
2 garlic cloves, crushed
0 tbsp harissa paste (see page 235)
a generous pinch of saffron threads
1 tsp salt
1 cinnamon stick
600ml (1 pint) chicken stock (see page 222)
75g (3oz) raisins
2 × 400g cans chickpeas, drained and rinsed
ground black pepper
plain naan or pitta bread to serve

1. Heat a large wide non-stick pan. Add the chicken pieces and fry until well browned all over. Add the butter and, when melted, add the onion and garlic. Cook, stirring, for 5 minutes.

2. Add the harissa, saffron, salt and cinnamon stick, then season well with pepper. Pour in the stock and bring to the boil. Reduce the heat, cover the pan and simmer gently for 25–30 minutes.

3. Add the raisins and chickpeas and bring to the boil, then reduce the heat and simmer, uncovered, for 5–10 minutes.

4. Serve with warm flatbread such as plain naan or pitta.

FREEZING TIP

To freeze Freeze leftover portions separately. Complete the recipe, then cool quickly. Put into a sealable container and freeze for up to three months.
To use Thaw overnight in the fridge. Put into a pan, cover and bring to the boil. Reduce the heat to low, then reheat for 40 minutes or until the chicken is hot right through.

Moroccan Spiced Chicken Kebabs

Preparation Time 10 minutes, plus marinating and soaking • Cooking Time 10–12 minutes • Serves 4 •
Per Serving 190 calories, 7g fat (of which 1g saturates), 1g carbohydrate, 0.2g salt • Gluten Free • Dairy Free • Easy

2 tbsp olive oil

15g (½oz) fresh flat-leafed parsley

1 garlic clove

½ tsp paprika

1 tsp ground cumin

zest and juice of 1 lemon

4 skinless chicken breasts, cut into bite-size chunks

salt

shredded lettuce, sliced cucumber and tomatoes, and lime wedges to serve

1. Put the oil into a blender and add the parsley, garlic, paprika, cumin, lemon zest and juice and a pinch of salt. Whiz to make a paste.

2. Put the chicken into a medium-sized shallow dish and rub in the spice paste. Leave to marinate for at least 20 minutes. Meanwhile, soak some wooden skewers in water and preheat the grill to high.

3. Thread the marinated chicken on to the skewers and grill for 10–12 minutes, turning every now and then, until the meat is cooked through. Serve with shredded lettuce, sliced cucumber and tomatoes, and lime wedges.

TRY SOMETHING DIFFERENT

Instead of chicken, use 700g (1½lb) lean lamb fillet or leg of lamb, cut into chunks.

Jambalaya

Preparation Time 15 minutes • Cooking Time about 50 minutes, plus standing • Serves 4 • Per Serving 558 calories, 25g fat (of which 6g saturates), 49g carbohydrate, 0g salt • Gluten Free • Dairy Free • Easy

2 tbsp olive oil

300g (11oz) boneless, skinless chicken thighs, cut into chunks

75g (3oz) French sausage, such as saucisse sèche, chopped

2 celery sticks, chopped

1 large onion, finely chopped

225g (8oz) long-grain rice

1 tbsp tomato purée

2 tsp Cajun spice mix

500ml (18fl oz) hot chicken stock (see page 222)

1 bay leaf

4 large tomatoes, roughly chopped

200g (7oz) raw tiger prawns, peeled and deveined (see Cook's Tip)

1. Heat 1 tbsp oil in a large pan. Add the chicken and sausage and fry over a medium heat until browned. Remove with a slotted spoon and put to one side.

2. Add the remaining oil to the pan with the celery and onion. Fry gently for 15 minutes or until the vegetables are softened but not coloured. Tip in the rice and stir for 1 minute to coat in the oil. Add the tomato purée and spice mix and cook for a further 2 minutes.

3. Pour in the hot stock and return the browned chicken and sausage to the pan with the bay leaf and chopped tomatoes. Simmer for 20–25 minutes until the stock has been fully absorbed and the rice is cooked.

4. Stir in the prawns and cover the pan. Leave to stand for 10 minutes or until the prawns have turned pink. Serve immediately.

COOK'S TIP

To devein prawns, using a small sharp knife, make a shallow cut along the back of the prawn. Using the point of the knife, remove and discard the black vein (intestinal tract) that runs along the back of the prawn.

Caribbean Chicken

Preparation Time 40 minutes, plus marinating • Cooking Time 45–50 minutes • Serves 5 • Per Serving 617 calories, 39g fat (of which 12g saturates), 25g carbohydrate, 2.1g salt • Easy

10 chicken pieces (such as thighs, drumsticks, wings or breasts), skinned

1 tsp salt

1 tbsp ground coriander

2 tsp ground cumin

1 tbsp paprika

a pinch of ground nutmeg

1 fresh Scotch bonnet or other hot red chilli, seeded and chopped (see Cook's Tips, page 8)

1 onion, chopped

5 fresh thyme sprigs

4 garlic cloves, crushed

2 tbsp dark soy sauce

juice of 1 lemon

2 tbsp vegetable oil

2 tbsp light muscovado sugar

350g (12oz) American easy-cook rice

3 tbsp dark rum (optional)

25g (1oz) butter

2 × 300g cans black-eye beans, drained

ground black pepper

a few freshly chopped thyme sprigs to garnish

1. Pierce the chicken pieces with a knife, put into a container and sprinkle with ½ tsp salt, some pepper, the coriander, cumin, paprika and nutmeg. Add the chilli, onion, thyme leaves and garlic. Pour the soy sauce and lemon juice over and stir to combine. Cover, chill and leave to marinate for at least 4 hours.

2. Heat a 3.4 litre (6 pint) heavy-based pan over a medium heat for 2 minutes. Add the oil and sugar and cook for 3 minutes or until it turns a golden caramel colour. (Don't overcook it as the mixture will blacken and taste burnt – watch it closely.) Remove the chicken from the marinade. Add to the caramel mixture. Cover and cook over a medium heat for 5 minutes. Turn the chicken and cook, covered, for another 5 minutes or until evenly browned. Add the onion mixture and any marinade juices. Turn again, then re-cover and cook for 10 minutes.

3. Add the rice and stir to combine with the chicken, then pour in 900ml (1½ pints) cold water. Add the rum, if using, the butter and the remaining ½ tsp salt. Cover and simmer over a gentle heat, without lifting the lid, for 20 minutes or until the rice is tender and most of the liquid has been absorbed.

4. Add the black-eye beans to the pan and mix well. Cover the pan and cook for 3–5 minutes until the beans are warmed through and all the liquid has been absorbed, taking care that the rice doesn't stick to the base of the pan. Garnish with the chopped thyme and serve hot.

Chicken Fajitas

Preparation Time 10 minutes • Cooking Time 20 minutes • Serves 4 • Per Serving 651 calories,
23g fat (of which 8g saturates), 63g carbohydrate, 1.6g salt • Easy

**700g (1½lb) boneless, skinless
  chicken breasts, cut into
  chunky strips**
2 tbsp fajita seasoning
1 tbsp sunflower oil
1 red pepper, seeded and sliced
360g jar fajita sauce
1 bunch of spring onions, halved
8 large flour tortillas
150g (5oz) tomato salsa
125g (4oz) guacamole dip
150ml (¼ pint) soured cream

1. Put the chicken breasts into a shallow dish and toss together with the fajita seasoning. Heat the oil in a large non-stick frying pan. Add the chicken and cook for 5 minutes or until golden brown and tender.

2. Add the red pepper and cook for 2 minutes. Pour in the fajita sauce and bring to the boil, then reduce the heat and simmer for 5 minutes or until thoroughly heated. Add a splash of boiling water if the sauce becomes too thick. Stir in the spring onions and cook for 2 minutes.

3. Meanwhile, warm the tortillas in a microwave on full power for 45 seconds, or wrap in foil and warm in a preheated oven at 180°C (160°C fan oven) mark 4 for 10 minutes.

4. Transfer the chicken to a serving dish and take to the table, along with the tortillas, salsa, guacamole and soured cream. Let everyone help themselves.

Chicken Falafels

Preparation Time 20 minutes, plus soaking • Cooking Time 20 minutes • Serves 4 • Per Serving 287 calories, 14g fat (of which 3g saturates), 10g carbohydrate, 1.1g salt • Dairy Free • Easy

450g (1lb) minced chicken
3 shallots, finely chopped
125g (4oz) canned chickpeas (about ½ can), drained and rinsed
2.5cm (1in) piece fresh root ginger, peeled and grated
½ tsp salt
20g (¾oz) freshly chopped coriander
1 medium egg
3 tbsp olive oil
400g can chopped tomatoes
1 tsp caster sugar

FOR THE COUSCOUS SALAD
200g (7oz) couscous
350ml (12fl oz) hot chicken stock (see page 222)
grated zest and juice of ½ lemon
25g (1oz) pinenuts
seeds from ½ pomegranate
3 tbsp extra virgin olive oil
2–3 tbsp freshly chopped parsley

1. First, make the couscous salad. Put the couscous into a bowl and add the hot stock and lemon zest. Leave to soak for 20 minutes. Meanwhile, toast the pinenuts in a dry pan, tossing regularly, until golden. Use a fork to fluff up the couscous, then stir in the pinenuts, pomegranate seeds, lemon juice, extra virgin olive oil and parsley.

2. Put the minced chicken into a food processor. Add 1 chopped shallot, the chickpeas, grated ginger and salt and whiz to combine.

3. Add the coriander and egg and whiz again briefly. With damp hands, shape into 12 balls, each measuring 6.5cm (2½in).

4. Heat 2 tbsp olive oil in a frying pan. Fry the patties for 2–3 minutes on each side until golden brown.

5. Meanwhile, fry the remaining shallots in a pan with the remaining olive oil. Stir in the tomatoes and sugar and simmer for 10 minutes or until slightly thickened. Serve the patties with the couscous salad, and with the sauce on the side.

Chicken Kebabs with Tabbouleh

Preparation Time 35 minutes, plus marinating and soaking • Cooking Time 10–12 minutes • Serves 4 •
Per Serving 330 calories, 8g fat (of which 1g saturates), 19g carbohydrate, 0.3g salt • Dairy Free • Easy

1 tbsp balsamic vinegar

6 tbsp olive oil

grated zest of 1 lime and juice of 2 limes

2 garlic cloves, crushed

4 large skinless chicken breasts, about 700g (1½lb), cut into 2.5cm (1in) cubes

75g (3oz) bulgur wheat

½ cucumber, halved lengthways, seeded and diced

4 plum tomatoes, seeded and diced

1 small red onion, finely chopped

4 tbsp freshly chopped mint

4 tbsp freshly chopped flat-leafed parsley

ground black pepper

lime wedges and mint sprigs to garnish

1. Whisk the balsamic vinegar, 3 tbsp oil, the zest and juice of 1 lime and 1 garlic clove together in a large bowl. Add the chicken, mix well, then cover, chill and leave to marinate for at least 2 hours, preferably overnight.

2. To make the tabbouleh, put the bulgur wheat into a bowl, cover with double its volume of boiling water and leave to soak for 15 minutes. Drain the bulgur wheat, squeeze out the liquid and put back into the bowl. Stir in the cucumber, tomatoes, onion and herbs and season with pepper.

3. Whisk the remaining oil, lime juice and garlic together in a small bowl. Add to the bulgur wheat and mix gently but thoroughly until the bulgur is well coated. Cover and chill in the fridge.

4. Preheat the barbecue, grill or griddle. Soak eight wooden skewers in water for 20 minutes. Remove the chicken from the marinade, thread on to the skewers and cook for 10–12 minutes, turning every now and then, or until cooked through. Serve with the tabbouleh, garnished with lime wedges and mint sprigs.

Chicken Satay Skewers

Preparation Time 30 minutes, plus chilling and soaking • Cooking Time 8–10 minutes • Serves 4 •
Per Serving 687 calories, 51g fat (of which 21g saturates), 11g carbohydrate, 2.1g salt • Gluten Free • Dairy Free • Easy

1 tbsp each coriander and
　cumin seeds
2 tsp ground turmeric
4 garlic cloves, roughly chopped
grated zest and juice of 1 lemon
2 bird's eye chillies, finely chopped
　(see Cook's Tips, page 8)
3 tbsp vegetable oil
4 boneless, skinless chicken
　breasts, about 550g (1¼lb),
　cut into finger-length strips
salt and ground black pepper
½ cucumber, cut into sticks
　to serve

FOR THE SATAY SAUCE
200g (7oz) salted peanuts
1 tbsp molasses sugar
½ lemongrass stalk, chopped
2 tbsp dark soy sauce
juice of ½ lime
200ml (7fl oz) coconut cream

1. Put the coriander and cumin seeds and the turmeric into a dry frying pan and heat for 30 seconds. Tip into a blender and add the garlic, lemon zest and juice, chillies, 1 tbsp oil and 1 tsp salt. Whiz for 1–2 minutes.

2. Put the paste into a large shallow dish, add the chicken and toss everything together. Cover and chill in the fridge for at least 20 minutes or up to 12 hours.

3. To make the satay sauce, put the peanuts, sugar, lemongrass, soy sauce, lime juice and coconut cream into a food processor and add 2 tbsp water. Whiz to make a thick chunky sauce, then spoon into a dish. Cover and chill.

4. Preheat the barbecue or grill until hot. Soak 24 bamboo skewers in water for 20 minutes. Thread the chicken on to the skewers, drizzle with the remaining oil and cook for 4–5 minutes on each side or until cooked through. Serve with the satay sauce and the cucumber.

TRY SOMETHING DIFFERENT
Replace the chicken with strips of pork tenderloin or beef rump.

Chicken Chow Mein

Preparation Time 10 minutes • Cooking Time 10 minutes • Serves 4 • Per Serving 451 calories,
11g fat (of which 2g saturates), 59g carbohydrate, 1.3g salt • Dairy Free • Easy

- **250g (9oz) medium egg noodles**
- **1 tbsp toasted sesame oil**
- **2 boneless, skinless chicken breasts, about 125g (4oz) each, cut into thin strips**
- **1 bunch of spring onions, thinly sliced diagonally**
- **150g (5oz) mangetouts, thickly sliced diagonally**
- **125g (4oz) bean sprouts**
- **100g (3½oz) cooked ham, finely shredded**
- **120g sachet chow mein sauce**
- **salt and ground black pepper**
- **light soy sauce to serve**

1. Cook the noodles in boiling water for 4 minutes or according to the pack instructions. Drain, rinse thoroughly in cold water, drain again and put to one side.

2. Meanwhile, heat a wok or large frying pan until hot, then add the oil. Add the chicken and stir-fry over a high heat for 3–4 minutes until browned all over. Add the spring onions and mangetouts and stir-fry for 2 minutes. Stir in the bean sprouts and ham and cook for a further 2 minutes.

3. Add the drained noodles, then pour the chow mein sauce into the pan and toss together to coat evenly. Stir-fry for 2 minutes or until piping hot. Season with salt and pepper and serve immediately with light soy sauce to drizzle over the chow mein.

Exotic Chicken

Preparation Time 20 minutes • Cooking Time 1¾ hours • Serves 6 • Per Serving 370 calories, 17g fat (of which 6g saturates), 22g carbohydrate, 0.5g salt • Easy

1 large red chilli, seeded and finely chopped (see Cook's Tips, page 8)
2.5cm (1in) piece fresh root ginger, peeled and thinly sliced
10cm (4in) piece lemongrass, cut into thin matchsticks
2 kaffir lime leaves (or a little extra grated lime zest), cut into thin matchsticks
grated zest of 1 lime
2 garlic bulbs, halved
2 tbsp freshly chopped coriander
1.8kg (4lb) oven-ready chicken
1 tbsp chilli sauce
3 tbsp rapeseed oil
1 tsp ground turmeric
800g (1¾lb) baby new potatoes
3 tbsp desiccated coconut
juice of 2 limes
salt and ground black pepper
fresh coriander to garnish

1. Preheat the oven to 200°C (180°C fan oven) mark 6. Cut two pieces of non-stick baking parchment, each measuring about 75 × 40cm (30 × 16in). Sprinkle each with water to dampen slightly, then put one on top of the other.

2. Combine the chilli, ginger, lemongrass, kaffir lime leaves, some grated lime zest and the garlic with the coriander. Pile in the centre of the baking parchment. Season inside the chicken generously with salt and pepper, then scatter the rest of the grated lime zest over and put the chicken on top of the spices.

3. Mix the chilli sauce with 1 tbsp oil and brush all over the chicken. Bring the edges of the baking parchment together and tie at the top with kitchen string to encase the chicken completely. Put into a large roasting tin just big enough to hold the parcel and cook in the oven for 1 hour 40 minutes.

4. Mix the remaining oil with the turmeric and potatoes in a roasting tin and toss well to coat evenly. Put on a tray above the chicken for the last 40 minutes of the cooking time. Roast until golden and tender. Remove the potatoes from the oven, add the desiccated coconut and stir to coat evenly. Put back in the oven and cook for a further 5 minutes or until the coconut has turned golden. Keep warm.

5. Untie the parcel and allow any juices inside the chicken to run into a pan. Lift the chicken out and add as much of the flavouring ingredients as possible to the pan. Cover the chicken with foil and keep warm in a low oven. Add the lime juice to the pan and bring to the boil. Bubble furiously for 1 minute. Keep hot.

6. Carve the chicken and serve with the roast potatoes and cooking juices. Garnish with fresh coriander.

HOT & SPICY

Chicken Enchiladas

Preparation Time 30 minutes • Cooking Time 45 minutes • Serves 6 • Per Serving 433 calories,
17g fat (of which 10g saturates), 37g carbohydrate, 1.3g salt • Easy

450g (1lb) skinless chicken breasts,
** cut into strips**
1 tsp dried oregano
1 tsp cumin seeds
5 tbsp olive oil, plus extra to oil
2 onions, finely chopped
125g (4oz) celery, cut into strips
2 garlic cloves, crushed
50g (2oz) sun-dried tomatoes in oil,
** drained and roughly chopped**

225g (8oz) brown-cap mushrooms,
** chopped**
250g (9oz) Cheddar, grated
2 tbsp freshly chopped coriander
2 tbsp lemon juice
6 flour tortillas
salt and ground black pepper
Salsa Verde to serve (see page 55)

1. Preheat the oven to 180°C (160°C fan oven) mark 4. Put the chicken into a bowl, add the oregano, cumin seeds and salt and pepper and toss to coat the chicken.

2. Heat half the oil in a large frying pan. Add the onions, celery and garlic and cook gently for 5–7 minutes. Add the tomatoes and mushrooms and cook for a further 2–3 minutes. Remove from the pan and put to one side.

3. Add the remaining oil to the pan and stir-fry the chicken in batches for 2–3 minutes. Add the chicken to the mushroom mixture, with 175g (6oz) cheese, the chopped coriander and lemon juice. Mix well and season with salt and pepper.

4. Divide the chicken mixture among the tortillas and roll up to enclose the filling. Put, seam side down, into an oiled ovenproof dish, then sprinkle with the remaining cheese. Cook in the oven for 25–30 minutes until golden and bubbling. Spoon the salsa verde over the enchiladas to serve.

Chicken Chilli

Preparation Time 20 minutes • Cooking Time 55 minutes • Serves 4 • Per Serving 350 calories,
12g fat (of which 3g saturates), 32g carbohydrate, 0.6g salt • Easy

2 × 20g packs fresh coriander
2 tbsp olive oil
1 large Spanish onion, finely
 chopped
1 red chilli, seeded and finely
 chopped (see Cook's Tips,
 page 8)
450g (1lb) chicken fillet, diced
1 tbsp plain flour

410g can mixed pulses or mixed
 beans, drained and rinsed
2 × 400g cans chopped tomatoes
 with garlic
1–2 tbsp light muscovado sugar
juice of 1 small lime
warm tortillas, grated Cheddar,
 chopped green chillies and
 soured cream to serve

1. Preheat the oven to 170°C
(150°C fan oven) mark 3. Chop
the leaves from the coriander stalks
and cut the stalks finely. Rewrap the
leaves and pop them in the fridge.

2. Heat 1 tbsp oil in a large
casserole. Add the onion, coriander
stalks and chilli and fry for 5–7
minutes or until the onion is soft
and golden. Spoon on to a plate and
put to one side.

3. Add the remaining oil to the
casserole. Add the chicken and fry
for 5 minutes or until golden.

4. Return the onion mixture to the
casserole and stir in the flour. Add
the pulses or beans, tomatoes and
sugar, then bring to the boil. Cover
with a tight-fitting lid and cook in
the oven for 40 minutes.

5. To serve, finely chop the
coriander leaves and stir most of
them into the casserole with the
lime juice. Serve with warm tortillas,
grated Cheddar, chopped green
chillies, the remaining coriander
and soured cream.

Chicken with Devilled Sauce

Preparation Time 20 minutes • Cooking Time 1 hour 50 minutes, plus resting • Serves 6 • Per Serving 652 calories, 48g fat (of which 17g saturates), 13g carbohydrate, 0.7g salt • Gluten Free • Easy

3 garlic cloves, chopped

1 large onion, chopped

2.3kg (5lb) chicken

450g (1lb) tomatoes, peeled, seeded and chopped

salt and ground black pepper

fresh basil sprigs to garnish

90ml (3fl oz) crème fraîche, warmed, to serve

FOR THE DEVILLED SAUCE

25g (1oz) butter

2 tbsp mango or sweet chutney, any large pieces chopped (see page 44)

2 tbsp Worcestershire sauce

2 tbsp wholegrain mustard

1 tsp paprika

3 tbsp freshly squeezed orange juice

1. Preheat the oven to 190°C (170°C fan oven) mark 5. To make the devilled sauce, melt the butter in a pan. Add the mango or sweet chutney, Worcestershire sauce, mustard, paprika, orange juice and salt and pepper and mix together.

2. Put the garlic and onion into the cavity of the chicken. Put the chicken into a large roasting tin and spoon over some of the devilled sauce. Roast the chicken in the oven, basting frequently with the sauce, for 1¾ hours or until the juices run clear when the thickest part of the thigh is pierced with a skewer. The skin should be slightly charred; if it's becoming too brown, cover it with foil towards the end of the cooking time.

3. Put the chicken on a warmed serving plate and keep warm. Skim off the fat from the juices in the roasting tin and discard, then stir the tomatoes into the juices with any remaining devilled sauce. Heat through and season with salt and pepper. Carve the chicken and serve with the devilled sauce and warmed crème fraîche. Garnish with basil.

TRY SOMETHING DIFFERENT
For a more fiery sauce, add a finely chopped chilli (see Cook's Tips, page 8) to the devilled mixture before basting.

Chicken with Spicy Couscous

Preparation Time 15 minutes, plus soaking • Serves 4 • Per Serving 223 calories,
6g fat (of which 2g saturates), 30g carbohydrate, 0.2g salt • Easy

125g (4oz) couscous
1 ripe mango, peeled, stoned and
   cut into 2.5cm (1in) chunks
1 tbsp lemon or lime juice
125g tub fresh tomato salsa
3 tbsp Mango Chutney
   (see page 44)
3 tbsp orange juice
2 tbsp freshly chopped coriander
200g (7oz) chargrilled chicken
   fillets
4 tbsp fromage frais (optional)
salt and ground black pepper
freshly chopped coriander and
   lime wedges to garnish

1. Put the couscous into a large bowl and pour 300ml (½ pint) boiling water over. Season well with salt and pepper, then leave to soak for 15 minutes.

2. Put the mango chunks on a large plate and sprinkle with the lemon or lime juice.

3. Mix the tomato salsa with the mango chutney, orange juice and coriander in a small bowl.

4. Drain the couscous if necessary, fluff the grains with a fork, then stir in the salsa mixture and check the seasoning. Turn out on to a large serving dish and arrange the chicken and mango on top.

5. Just before serving, spoon the fromage frais over the chicken, if you like, then garnish with chopped coriander and lime wedges.

Fiery Mango Chicken

Preparation Time 15 minutes, plus marinating • Cooking Time 10 minutes • Serves 4 • Per Serving 220 calories, 8g fat (of which 2g saturates), 7g carbohydrate, 0.3g salt • Gluten Free • Easy

4 tbsp hot mango chutney or ordinary Mango Chutney (see page 282), plus ½ tsp Tabasco

grated zest and juice of 1 lime

4 tbsp natural yogurt

2 tbsp freshly chopped coriander

1 small green chilli (optional), seeded and finely chopped (see Cook's Tips, page 10)

4 chicken breasts, with skin

1 large ripe mango, peeled and stoned

oil to brush

salt and ground black pepper

fresh coriander sprigs and lime wedges to garnish

1. Mix together the chutney, lime zest and juice, yogurt, chopped coriander and, if you like it spicy, the finely chopped chilli.

2. Put the chicken breasts, skin side down, on the worksurface, cover with clingfilm and lightly beat with a rolling pin. Slice each into three pieces and put into the yogurt mixture and stir to coat. Cover the bowl, chill and leave to marinate for at least 30 minutes or overnight.

3. Preheat the barbecue or grill. Slice the mango into four thick pieces. Brush lightly with oil and season well with salt and pepper. Cook for about 2 minutes on each side – the fruit should be lightly charred but still firm. Put to one side.

4. Cook the chicken for 3–5 minutes on each side until golden brown. Serve with the cooked mango, garnished with coriander sprigs and lime wedges.

Spiced Tikka Kebabs

Preparation Time 10 minutes • Cooking Time 20 minutes • Serves 4 • Per Serving 150 calories,
5g fat (of which 1g saturates), 4g carbohydrate, 0.3g salt • Gluten Free • Easy

2 tbsp tikka paste
150g (5oz) natural yogurt
juice of ½ lime
4 spring onions, chopped
**350g (12oz) skinless chicken, cut
into bite-size pieces**
**lime wedges and Mixed Salad (see
Cook's Tip) to serve**

1. Preheat the grill. Put the tikka paste, yogurt, lime juice and spring onions into a large bowl. Add the chicken and toss well. Thread the chicken on to metal skewers.

2. Grill the chicken for 8–10 minutes on each side, turning and basting with the paste, until cooked through. Serve with lime wedges to squeeze over the kebabs, and mixed salad.

COOK'S TIP
Mixed Salad
Put 75g (3oz) green salad leaves into a large bowl. Add ¼ chopped avocado, a handful of halved cherry tomatoes, ½ chopped cucumber and the juice of 1 lime. Season to taste with salt and pepper and mix together.

Creamy Curried Chicken

Preparation Time 15 minutes • Cooking Time 30–35 minutes • Serves 4 • Per Serving 380 calories,
21g fat (of which 7g saturates), 9g carbohydrate, 0.9g salt • Easy

25g (1oz) butter

**700g (1½lb) skinless chicken
    breast fillets, cut into bite-size
    pieces**

1 small onion, chopped

4 celery sticks, chopped

**2 tbsp each mild curry paste and
    Mango Chutney (see page 44)**

2 tbsp lemon juice

**2 tbsp each Greek-style natural
    yogurt and mayonnaise**

3 tbsp milk

fresh flat-leafed parsley to garnish

rice to serve

1. Heat the butter in a pan. Add the chicken and fry for 15–20 minutes until cooked, then put to one side. Add the onion and celery to the pan and fry for 5 minutes until soft.

2. Stir in the curry paste, chutney and lemon juice and cook, stirring, for 2 minutes.

3. Take the pan off the heat, add the yogurt, mayonnaise and milk and stir well.

4. Put the chicken back into the pan and bring to simmering point. Cook until piping hot. Divide among four plates, garnish with parsley and serve with rice.

Thai Red Chicken Curry

Preparation Time 20 minutes • Cooking Time 18–25 minutes • Serves 6 • Per Serving 247 calories,
8g fat (of which 3g saturates), 15g carbohydrate, 1.2g salt • Gluten free • Dairy free • Easy

3 tbsp vegetable oil
450g (1lb) onions, finely chopped
200g (7oz) green beans, trimmed
125g (4oz) baby sweetcorn, cut on
 the diagonal
2 red peppers, seeded and cut into
 thick strips
1 tbsp Thai red curry paste, or
 to taste
1 red chilli, seeded and finely
 chopped (see Cook's Tips,
 page 8)
1 lemongrass stalk, very finely
 chopped
4 kaffir lime leaves, bruised
2 tbsp fresh root ginger, peeled and
 finely chopped
1 garlic clove, crushed
400ml can coconut milk
600ml (1 pint) chicken stock
450g (1lb) cooked chicken, cut
 into strips
150g (5oz) bean sprouts
fresh basil leaves to garnish

1. Heat the oil in a wok or large frying pan. Add the onions and cook for 4–5 minutes until soft.

2. Add the beans, baby sweetcorn and peppers to the pan and stir-fry for 3–4 minutes. Add the curry paste, chilli, lemongrass, kaffir lime leaves, ginger and garlic and cook for a further 2 minutes, stirring. Remove from the pan and put to one side.

3. Add the coconut milk and stock to the pan, bring to the boil and bubble vigorously for 5–10 minutes until reduced by one-quarter. Return the vegetables to the pan with the chicken and bean sprouts. Bring to the boil, then reduce the heat and simmer for 1–2 minutes until heated through. Serve immediately, garnished with basil leaves.

COOK'S TIP

This is a great way to use leftover chicken.

Chicken Curry with Rice

Preparation Time 20 minutes • Cooking Time 30 minutes, plus standing • Serves 4 • Per Serving 453 calories, 12g fat (of which 2g saturates), 49g carbohydrate, 2.4g salt • Gluten Free • Dairy Free • Easy

2 tbsp vegetable oil
1 onion, finely sliced
2 garlic cloves, crushed
6 boneless, skinless chicken
    thighs, cut into strips
2 tbsp tikka masala curry paste
200g can chopped tomatoes
450ml (¾ pint) hot vegetable stock
200g (7oz) basmati rice
1 tsp salt
225g (8oz) baby leaf spinach
poppadums and Mango Chutney
    (see page 44) to serve

1. Heat the oil in a large pan. Add the onion and fry over a medium heat for about 5 minutes or until golden. Add the garlic and chicken and stir-fry for about 5 minutes or until golden.

2. Add the curry paste, tomatoes and hot stock. Stir and bring to the boil, then reduce the heat, cover the pan and simmer over a low heat for 15 minutes or until the chicken is cooked (cut a piece in half to check that it's white all the way through).

3. Meanwhile, cook the rice. Put 600ml (1 pint) water into a medium pan, cover and bring to the boil. Add the rice and salt and stir. Replace the lid and reduce the heat to its lowest setting. Cook according to the pack instructions. Once cooked, cover with a teatowel and the lid. Leave for 5 minutes to absorb the steam.

4. Add the spinach to the curry and cook until it has just wilted.

5. Spoon the rice into bowls, add the curry and serve with poppadums and mango chutney.

Hot Jungle Curry

Preparation Time 10 minutes • Cooking Time 18–20 minutes • Serves 4 • Per Serving 160 calories,
5g fat (of which 1g saturates), 5g carbohydrate, 1.1g salt • Gluten Free • Dairy Free • Easy

1 tbsp vegetable oil

350g (12oz) boneless, skinless chicken breasts, cut into 5cm (2in) strips

2 tbsp Thai red curry paste

2.5cm (1in) piece fresh root ginger, peeled and thinly sliced

125g (4oz) aubergine, cut into bite-size pieces

125g (4oz) baby sweetcorn, halved lengthways

75g (3oz) green beans, trimmed

75g (3oz) button or brown-cap mushrooms, halved if large

2–3 kaffir lime leaves (optional)

450ml (¾ pint) chicken stock (see page 222)

2 tbsp Thai fish sauce

grated zest of ½ lime, plus extra to garnish

1 tsp tomato purée

1 tbsp soft brown sugar

rice to serve

1. Heat the oil in a wok or large frying pan. Add the chicken and cook, stirring, for 5 minutes or until the chicken turns golden brown.

2. Add the curry paste and cook for a further 1 minute. Add the ginger, aubergine, sweetcorn, beans, mushrooms and lime leaves, if using, and stir until coated in the curry paste. Add the remaining ingredients and bring to the boil. Reduce the heat and simmer for 10–12 minutes or until the chicken and vegetables are tender..Sprinkle with lime zest and serve with rice.

TRY SOMETHING DIFFERENT

Add a drained 225g can of bamboo shoots with the other vegetables in step 2, if you like.

Chicken, Bean & Spinach Curry

Preparation Time 10 minutes • Cooking Time about 20 minutes • Serves 4 • Per Serving 364 calories, 9g fat (of which 1g saturates), 41g carbohydrate, 2.9g salt • Gluten Free • Easy

1 tbsp sunflower oil

350g (12oz) boneless, skinless chicken breasts, cut into strips

1 garlic clove, crushed

300–350g tub or jar curry sauce

400g can aduki beans, drained and rinsed

175g (6oz) ready-to-eat dried apricots

150g (5oz) natural yogurt, plus extra to serve

125g (4oz) baby spinach leaves

naan bread to serve (optional)

1. Heat the oil in a large pan over a medium heat. Add the chicken strips and garlic and fry until golden. Add the curry sauce, aduki beans and apricots, then cover and simmer gently for 15 minutes or until the chicken is tender.

2. Over a low heat, stir in the yogurt, keeping the curry hot without boiling it, then stir in the spinach until it just begins to wilt. Add a spoonful of yogurt and serve with naan bread, if you like.

TRY SOMETHING DIFFERENT

Use pork escalopes, cut into thin strips, instead of chicken.

Chicken Tikka Masala

Preparation Time 15 minutes • Cooking Time 30 minutes • Serves 4 • Per Serving 297 calories, 17g fat (of which 4g saturates), 4g carbohydrate, 0.6g salt • Dairy Free • Easy

2 tbsp vegetable oil
1 onion, finely sliced
2 garlic cloves, crushed
6 boneless, skinless chicken
   thighs, cut into strips
2 tbsp tikka masala curry paste
200g can chopped tomatoes
450ml (¾ pint) hot vegetable stock
225g (8oz) baby spinach leaves
fresh coriander leaves to garnish
basmati rice, Mango Chutney
   (see page 44) and poppadoms
   to serve

1. Heat the oil in a large pan. Add the onion and fry over a medium heat for 5–7 minutes until golden. Add the garlic and chicken strips and stir-fry for about 5 minutes or until golden.

2. Stir in the curry paste, then add the tomatoes and hot stock. Bring to the boil, then reduce the heat, cover the pan and simmer over a low heat for 15 minutes or until the chicken is cooked through.

3. Add the spinach to the curry, stir and cook until the leaves have just wilted. Garnish with coriander and serve with rice, mango chutney and poppadoms.

Chicken Tikka with Coconut Dressing

Preparation Time 10 minutes • Serves 4 • Per Serving 493 calories, 17g fat (of which 9g saturates), 53g carbohydrate, 1.1g salt • Easy

125ml (4fl oz) crème fraîche
5 tbsp coconut milk
4 pitta breads
200g (7oz) mixed salad leaves
400g (14oz) cooked chicken tikka fillets, sliced
2 spring onions, finely sliced
2 tbsp Mango Chutney (see page 44)
15g (½oz) flaked almonds
25g (1oz) raisins

1. Mix the crème fraîche and coconut milk together in a bowl and put to one side.

2. Split each pitta bread to form a pocket, then fill each pocket with a generous handful of salad leaves. Divide the chicken among the pitta breads. Sprinkle some spring onion over the chicken, add the mango chutney and drizzle with the crème fraîche mixture. Top with a sprinkling of flaked almonds and raisins. Serve immediately.

Chicken & Coconut Curry

Preparation Time 15 minutes • Cooking Time 35 minutes • Serves 6 • Per Serving 204 calories,
6g fat (of which 1g saturates), 10g carbohydrate, 1.5g salt • Gluten Free • Dairy Free • Easy

2 garlic cloves, peeled
1 onion, quartered
1 lemongrass stalk, trimmed and halved
2.5cm (1in) piece fresh root ginger, peeled and halved
2 small hot chillies (see Cook's Tips, page 8)
a small handful of fresh coriander
1 tsp ground coriander
grated zest and juice of 1 lime

2 tbsp vegetable oil
6 boneless, skinless chicken breasts, each cut into three pieces
2 large tomatoes, peeled and chopped
2 tbsp Thai fish sauce
900ml (1½ pints) coconut milk
salt and ground black pepper
finely sliced red chilli to garnish
basmati rice to serve

1. Put the garlic, onion, lemongrass, ginger, chillies, fresh coriander, ground coriander and lime zest and juice into a food processor and whiz to a paste. Add a little water if the mixture gets stuck under the blades.

2. Heat the oil in a wok or large frying pan. Add the spice paste and cook over a fairly high heat for 3–4 minutes, stirring constantly. Add the chicken and cook for 5 minutes, stirring to coat in the spice mixture.

3. Add the tomatoes, fish sauce and coconut milk. Cover and simmer for about 25 minutes or until the chicken is cooked. Season with salt and pepper, garnish with red chilli and serve with basmati rice.

Easy Thai Red Curry

Preparation Time 5 minutes • Cooking Time 20 minutes • Serves 4 • Per Serving 248 calories, 8g fat (of which 1g saturates), 16g carbohydrate, 1g salt • Dairy Free • Easy

1 tbsp vegetable oil

3 tbsp Thai red curry paste

4 skinless chicken breasts, about 600g (1lb 5oz) total weight, sliced

400ml can coconut milk

300ml (½ pint) hot chicken (see page 222) or vegetable stock

juice of 1 lime, plus lime halves to serve

200g pack mixed baby sweetcorn and mangetouts

2 tbsp freshly chopped coriander, plus sprigs to garnish

rice or rice noodles to serve

1. Heat the oil in a wok or large frying pan over a low heat. Add the curry paste and cook for 2 minutes or until fragrant.

2. Add the sliced chicken and fry gently for about 10 minutes or until the chicken is browned.

3. Add the coconut milk, hot stock, lime juice and baby sweetcorn to the pan and bring to the boil. Add the mangetouts, then reduce the heat and simmer for 4–5 minutes until the chicken is cooked. Stir in the chopped coriander, garnish with coriander sprigs and serve immediately with rice or noodles, and lime halves to squeeze over.

Thai Green Curry

Preparation Time 10 minutes • Cooking Time 15 minutes • Serves 6 • Per Serving 132 calories, 2g fat (of which 0g saturates), 4g carbohydrate, 1.4g salt • Dairy Free • Easy

2 tsp vegetable oil

1 green chilli, seeded and finely chopped (see Cook's Tips, page 8)

4cm (1½in) piece fresh root ginger, peeled and finely grated

1 lemongrass stalk, trimmed and cut into three pieces

225g (8oz) brown-cap or oyster mushrooms

1 tbsp Thai green curry paste

300ml (½ pint) coconut milk

150ml (¼ pint) chicken stock (see page 222)

1 tbsp Thai fish sauce

1 tsp light soy sauce

350g (12oz) boneless, skinless chicken breasts, cut into bite-size pieces

350g (12oz) cooked peeled large prawns

fresh coriander sprigs to garnish

Thai rice (see page 141) to serve

1. Heat the oil in a wok or large frying pan. Add the chilli, ginger, lemongrass and mushrooms and stir-fry for about 3 minutes or until the mushrooms begin to turn golden. Add the curry paste and fry for a further 1 minute.

2. Pour in the coconut milk, stock, fish sauce and soy sauce and bring to the boil. Stir in the chicken, then reduce the heat and simmer for about 8 minutes or until the chicken is cooked.

3. Add the prawns and cook for a further 1 minute. Garnish with coriander sprigs and serve immediately with Thai rice.

Thai Poached Chicken

Preparation Time 10 minutes • Cooking Time 1½ hours • Serves 4 • Per Serving 579 calories,
36g fat (of which 10g saturates), 1g carbohydrate, 1g salt • Gluten Free • Dairy Free • Easy

2 limes, halved
1.4kg (3lb) chicken
a knob of butter
2 lemongrass stalks, crushed
450ml (¾ pint) dry white wine
450ml (¾ pint) chicken stock (see
page 222)
1 small bunch of coriander,
chopped
salt and ground black pepper
rice and vegetables to serve

1. Preheat the oven to 200°C (180°C fan oven) mark 6. Put 2 lime halves into the cavity of the chicken. Rub the chicken with the butter and season with salt and pepper. Put the chicken into a flameproof casserole.

2. Add the lemongrass and remaining lime to the casserole, then pour in the wine and stock. Cover with a tight-fitting lid and cook in the oven for 1 hour.

3. Uncover and cook for a further 30 minutes or until the chicken is cooked and the juices run clear when the thickest part of the thigh is pierced with a skewer. Sprinkle the coriander over the chicken and serve with rice and vegetables.

Chilli-fried Chicken with Coconut Noodles

Preparation Time 15–20 minutes • Cooking Time 15 minutes • Serves 6 • Per Serving 580 calories, 29g fat (of which 8g saturates), 37g carbohydrate, 3.2g salt • Dairy Free • Easy

2 tbsp plain flour

1 tsp mild chilli powder

1 tsp ground ginger

½ tsp salt

1 tsp caster sugar

6 boneless, skinless chicken breasts, about 150g (5oz) each, cut diagonally into three

250g (9oz) thread egg noodles

3 tbsp groundnut oil

1 large bunch of spring onions, sliced

1½ tsp Thai red curry paste or tandoori paste (see page 235)

150g (5oz) salted roasted peanuts, finely chopped

6 tbsp coconut milk

1. Mix the flour, chilli powder, ground ginger, salt and sugar in a bowl. Dip the chicken into the spiced flour and coat well.

2. Cook the noodles in boiling water according to the pack instructions, then drain.

3. Heat the oil in a frying pan. Add the chicken and fry for 5 minutes or until cooked. Put to one side, cover and keep warm. Add the spring onions to the pan and fry for 1 minute. Put to one side and keep warm.

4. Add the curry paste to the pan with 75g (3oz) peanuts and fry for 1 minute. Add the noodles and fry for 1 minute. Stir in the coconut milk and toss the noodles over a high heat for 30 seconds.

5. Put the chicken and spring onions on the coconut noodles. Scatter with the remaining peanuts and serve.

COOK'S TIP

Coconut milk gives a thick creaminess to stir-fries, soups and curries.

Spiced One-pot Chicken

Preparation Time 10 minutes, plus marinating • Cooking Time 1 hour 10 minutes • Serves 6 •
Per Serving 604 calories, 36g fat (of which 10g saturates), 20g carbohydrate, 0.5g salt • Dairy Free • Easy

3 tbsp Thai red curry paste
150ml (¼pint) orange juice
2 garlic cloves, crushed
6 chicken pieces, 2.3kg (5lb) total
  weight, with bone in
700g (1½lb) squash or pumpkin,
  peeled and cut into 5cm
  (2in) cubes
5 red onions, quartered
2 tbsp capers, drained and chopped
salt and ground black pepper

1. Combine the curry paste, orange juice and garlic in a bowl. Put the chicken pieces in the marinade and leave to marinate for 15 minutes.

2. Preheat the oven to 220°C (200°C fan oven) mark 7. Put the vegetables into a large roasting tin, then remove the chicken from the marinade and arrange on top of the vegetables. Pour the marinade over and season with salt and pepper. Mix everything together, so that it's covered with the marinade, then scatter with the capers.

3. Cook in the oven for 1 hour 10 minutes, turning from time to time, or until the chicken is cooked through and the skin is golden.

GET AHEAD

To prepare ahead *Complete the recipe to the end of step 2. Cover and chill for up to one day.*
To use *Complete the recipe, but cook for a further 5–10 minutes.*

BASICS

Preparing stock

Uncooked chicken bones can be used for stock: put the bones to one side when you joint a chicken, or ask your butcher to set some bones aside for you. If the chicken has not been previously frozen, the bones can be kept in a sealed plastic bag in the freezer. Alternatively, use the leftover carcass of a roast chicken.

Chicken Stock

For 1.1 litres (2 pints), you will need:
1.6kg (3½lb) chicken bones,
225g (8oz) each onions and celery,
sliced, 150g (5oz) chopped leeks,
1 bouquet garni (see Cook's Tip,
page 26), 1 tsp black peppercorns,
½ tsp salt.

1. Put all the ingredients into a large pan and add 3 litres (5¼ pints) cold water. Bring slowly to the boil and skim the surface.

2. Partially cover the pan, reduce the heat and simmer gently for 2 hours. Adjust the seasoning if necessary.

3. Strain the stock through a muslin-lined sieve into a bowl and cool quickly. Degrease (see right) before using.

COOK'S TIPS

• *To get a clearer liquid when making poultry stock, strain the cooked stock through four layers of muslin in a sieve.*
• *Stock will keep for three days in the fridge. If you want to keep it for a further three days, transfer it to a pan and reboil gently for 5 minutes. Leave to cool, put into a clean bowl and chill for a further three days.*
• *When making chicken stock, make sure there is a good ratio of meat to bones. The more meat you use, the more flavour the stock will have.*

Giblet Stock

To make 1.3 litres (2¼ pints), you
* will need:*
turkey giblets, 1 onion, quartered,
1 carrot, halved, 1 celery stick,
halved, 6 black peppercorns, 1 bay
leaf.

1. Put all the ingredients into a large pan and add 1.4 litres (2½ pints) cold water. Cover and bring to the boil.

Degreasing stock

Poultry stock needs to be degreased. You can mop the fat from the surface using kitchen paper, but the following methods are easier and more effective. There are three main methods that you can use: ladling, pouring and chilling.

1. Ladling While the stock is warm, place a ladle on the surface. Press down and allow the fat floating on the surface to trickle over the edge until the ladle is full. Discard the fat, then repeat until all the fat has been removed.

2. Pouring For this you need a degreasing jug or a double-pouring gravy boat, which has the spout at the base of the vessel. When you fill the jug or gravy boat with a fatty liquid, the fat rises. When you pour, the stock comes out while the fat stays behind in the jug.

2. Reduce the heat, then simmer for 30 minutes–1 hour, skimming occasionally.

3. Strain the stock through a muslin-lined sieve into a bowl and cool quickly. Put into a sealable container and chill for up to three days.

3. Chilling Put the stock into the fridge until the fat solidifies, then remove the pieces of fat using a slotted spoon.

Preparing the bird for cooking

Chicken and other poultry and game birds may be bought whole for roasting, or in pieces ready for cooking. It is often cheaper to buy a whole bird, then joint it yourself for cooking as required.

All chickens and turkeys are jointed in much of the same way. The only difference is the size. To prepare chicken and other poultry for cooking you will need a sharp meat knife, poultry shears to cut the bones and a trussing needle.

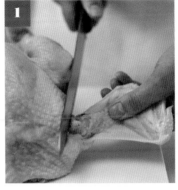

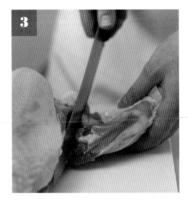

Jointing

1. Using a sharp meat knife with a curved blade, cut out the wishbone, then cut off the wings in a single piece. Remove the wing tips.

2. With the tail pointing towards you and the breast side up, pull one leg away and cut through the skin between the leg and breast. Pull the leg down until you crack the joint between the thigh bone and ribcage.

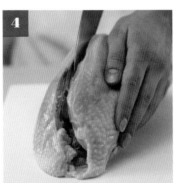

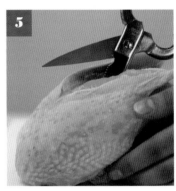

3. Cut through that joint, then cut through the remaining leg meat. Repeat on the other side.

4. To remove the breast without any bone, make a cut along the length of the breastbone. Gently teasing the flesh away from the ribs with the knife, work the blade down between the flesh and ribs of one breast and cut it off neatly. (Always cut in, towards the bone.) Repeat on the other side.

5. To remove the breast with bone in, make a cut along the full length of the breastbone. Using poultry shears, cut through the breastbone, then cut through the ribcage following the outline of the breast meat. Repeat on the other side. Trim off any flaps of skin or fat.

Trussing

When roasting poultry, it is not necessary to truss it but it gives the bird a neater shape for serving at the table.

1. Cut out the wishbone by pulling back the flap of skin at the neck end and locating the tip of the bone with a small sharp knife. Run the knife along the inside of the bone on both sides, then on the outside. Take care not to cut deep into the breast meat. Use poultry shears or sharp-pointed scissors to snip the tip of the bone from the breastbone and pull the bone away from the breast. Snip the two ends or pull them out by hand.

2. Pull off any loose fat from the neck or cavity. Put the wing tips under the breast and fold the neck flap on to the back of the bird. Thread a trussing needle and use it to secure the neck flap.

3. Push a metal skewer through both legs, at the joint between thigh and drumstick. Twist some string around both ends of the skewer and pull firmly to tighten.

4. Turn the bird over. Bring the string over the ends of the drumsticks, pull tight and tie to secure the legs.

Skinning breast fillets

1. Firmly grab the flap of skin at the small end of the breast and pull towards the other end of the breast. Remove the skin and discard, then prepare or cook the fillet as required.

Slicing breast fillets

1. Cut or pull out the long strip of flesh lying on the inside of the fillet. Slice it across the grain to the thickness required for your recipe. (Raw chicken should not be cut less than about 3mm/⅛in thick.)

2. Starting at the small tip of the breast, cut slices of the required thickness. Alternatively, cut into chunks or dice.

Cutting escalopes

Escalopes are good for quick frying.

1. Cut or pull out the long strip of flesh lying on the inside of the fillet. (It can be used for stir-fries, stuffings, etc.)

2. Pressing the breast firmly on to the chopping board with the flat of one hand, carve a thin slice from underneath the breast using a sharp knife. (The knife blade should be parallel with the chopping board.) Remove that slice, then repeat until the breast meat is too small to slice.

3. To make escalopes, put the slices of chicken between two sheets of clingfilm or greaseproof paper and pound them with a meat mallet until they are about 3mm (⅛in) thick.

Spatchcocking

A technique to flatten smaller poultry and guinea fowl for grilling.

1. Hold the bird on a board, breast down. Cut through one side of the backbone with poultry shears. Repeat on other side and remove.

2. Turn bird over, press down until you hear breastbone crack. Thread skewers through legs and breasts.

Boning

Boned poultry, stuffed and roasted, makes an attractive dish.

1. Using a meat knife with a curved blade, remove the wishbone (see step 1, page 223) and the first two sections of the wings.

2. Lay the chicken breast side down with the back facing up, and cut down to the backbone along the whole length of the bird. Pulling skin and flesh away as you go, work a sharp knife between the flesh and bone down one side of the bird. Always cut in, towards the bone.

3. You will soon reach the joints connecting the thigh and wing to the body. Cut through both joints, taking care not to cut through the skin. Do not pierce the skin; it will be the casing for your cooked dish. Continue cutting down between the breast meat and ribcage, again taking care to cut towards the bone.

4. When you reach the tip of the breastbone, turn the bird around and repeat on the other side. Cut through the soft cartilage along the length of the breastbone to remove the boned flesh in a single piece.

5. To remove the wings and legs, cut the tendons at the end of the bones and then use a small chopping knife to scrape off the flesh along the full length of bone. Pull out the bone. Do this twice with the legs to remove the thigh and drumstick.

HYGIENE

- Raw poultry contains harmful bacteria that can spread easily to anything they touch.
- Always wash your hands, kitchen surfaces, chopping boards, knives and equipment before and after handling poultry.
- Don't let raw poultry touch other foods.
- Always cover raw poultry and store in the bottom of the fridge, where it can't touch or drip on to other foods.

Cooking chicken & other poultry

Deep-frying

1. Prepare the poultry for frying and chill in the fridge. Prepare the seasoned flour, batter or coating. Heat vegetable oil in a deep-fryer to 180°C (test by frying a small cube of bread; it should brown in 40 seconds). Start battering or coating each piece of poultry.

2. Using tongs, carefully lower the poultry into the oil. Don't add more than three or four pieces at a time (otherwise the temperature will drop and the poultry will take longer to cook and become greasy). Deep-fry small chunks or strips for about 10 minutes, jointed pieces for about 15 minutes.

3. As the pieces become golden and crisp, remove them with a slotted spoon and drain on kitchen paper. Sprinkle with a little salt and serve immediately, or keep warm in the oven until everything is cooked.

COOK'S TIPS

• *Coat each piece of food well and make sure that they are completely covered in the coating.*
• *To speed up the cooking time, cut the chicken into strips or chunks.*

Pot-roasting

To serve four to six, you will need:
2 tbsp vegetable oil, 1 onion, cut into wedges, 2 rashers rindless streaky bacon, chopped, 1.4–1.6kg (3–3½lb) chicken, 2 small turnips, cut into wedges, 6 carrots, halved, 1 crushed garlic clove, 1 bouquet garni (see page Cook's Tip, page 26), 600ml (1 pint) chicken stock, 100ml (3½fl oz) dry white wine, a small handful of freshly chopped parsley, salt and ground black pepper.

1. Preheat the oven to 200°C (180°C fan oven) mark 6. Heat the oil in a flameproof casserole. Add the onion and bacon and fry for 5 minutes. Put to one side. Add the chicken and brown all over for 10 minutes, then put to one side. Fry the turnips, carrots and garlic for 2 minutes, then put the bacon, onion and chicken back into the casserole.

2. Add the bouquet garni, stock, wine and season and bring to the boil. Cook in the oven, basting now and then, for 1 hour 20 minutes or until the juices run clear when the thigh is pierced with a sharp knife. Stir in the parsley and carve.

Casseroling

To serve four to six, you will need:
1 jointed chicken (see page 223), 3 tbsp vegetable oil, 1 chopped onion, 2 crushed garlic cloves, 2 each chopped celery sticks and carrots, 1 tbsp plain flour, 2 tbsp freshly chopped tarragon or thyme, chicken stock and/or wine, salt and ground black pepper.

1. Preheat the oven to 180°C (160°C fan oven) mark 4. Cut the chicken legs and breasts in half.

2. Heat the oil in a flameproof casserole and brown the chicken all over. Remove from the casserole and pour off the excess oil. Add the onion and garlic and brown for a few minutes. Add the vegetables, then stir in the flour and cook for 1 minute. Add the herbs and season. Add the chicken and pour in the stock and/or wine to come three-quarters of the way up the poultry. Cook in the oven for 1–1½ hours or until the chicken is cooked through.

PERFECT POT-ROASTS

• Pot-roasting is the perfect way to cook almost any poultry or game bird apart from duck or goose, which are too fatty and do not give good results, and turkey, which are too large to fit in the average casserole dish.
• Make sure that you use a large enough casserole and that the bird doesn't fit too closely to the sides of the dish.
• Watch out for overcooking – the closed pot cooks birds almost as fast as an ordinary roast chicken in the oven would cook.
• Check the liquid level in the casserole from time to time. If it's too dry, add a little more. Water is fine, stock or wine are even better.
• Timings for pot-roasted poultry: about 45 minutes for small birds such as poussin, or 1–1½ hours for chicken or guinea fowl.

Poaching

The quick and gentle method of poaching will produce a light broth.

1. Brown the bird in oil if you wish (this is not necessary but will give a deeper flavour), then transfer to a pan that will hold it easily: a large frying pan or sauté pan is good for pieces, a large pan or casserole for a whole bird.

2. Add 1 roughly chopped onion, 2 crushed garlic cloves, 2 chopped carrots, 2 chopped celery sticks, 6 whole black peppercorns and 1 tsp dried mixed herbs, scattering them about the whole bird or between the pieces. Pour in just enough stock to cover, then simmer, uncovered, for about 1 hour (for a whole bird) or 30–40 minutes (for pieces).

3. Gently lift the bird out of the liquid. If you are planning to use the liquid as the basis for a sauce, reduce it by at least half.

COOK'S TIPS
● *Don't rush the cooking by using a very high heat. If you need to speed things up, cover the pan during the first half of cooking.*
● *Don't let the poultry cook for too long, as it can quickly dry out and toughen over a high heat.*

Pan-frying

This is a quick method for cooking chicken pieces and you can make a sauce with the pan juices at the end, if you like.

1. Pour in enough oil (or a mixture of oil and clarified butter) to fill a frying pan to a depth of about 5mm (¼ in) and put the pan over a medium heat.

2. Season the chicken with salt and ground black pepper, then carefully add to the pan, flesh side down, and fry for 10–15 minutes until it's browned. (Don't put too many pieces of chicken in the pan at once or the chicken will cook partly in its own steam.)

3. Turn the pieces over and cook on the skin side for a further 10–15 minutes until the skin is brown and the flesh is cooked but still juicy all the way through.

4. Remove the chicken from the pan using a pair of tongs and keep warm. Pour off the excess oil and deglaze the pan with a little wine or stock. Stir thoroughly, scraping up the sediment, then add some herbs and finely chopped garlic or onion and cook for a few minutes. Serve the chicken with the sauce.

Steaming

1. Cut the chicken into thick shreds or chunks, or use thighs, drumsticks or halved breasts. Marinate (see page 233), if you like, for at least 1 hour.

2. Arrange the chicken in a single layer on a heatproof dish that is small enough to fit inside the steamer. Place in the steamer, cover and steam for 20–40 minutes until just cooked through.

Grilling

This method is perfect for cooking pieces such as breast fillets or for strips or chunks threaded on to skewers. Small birds can be spatchcocked (see page 224) and grilled.

1. Marinate (see page 233) the chicken pieces for 30 minutes, then drain and pat dry. Alternatively, brush the chicken with a flavoured oil (see page 233). Put the pieces on a wire rack over a grill pan or roasting tin and set the pan under a preheated grill so that it is about 8cm (3¼ in) from the heat source.

2. Every few minutes brush a little of the marinade or a teaspoon of oil over the chicken.

3. When cooked on one side, turn with tongs and cook the other side until cooked through. Avoid piercing the flesh when turning. Allow 12–20 minutes for a breast fillet or kebabs and 20–30 minutes for a spatchcocked bird.

Stir-frying

1. Cut the chicken into small, even-sized strips or dice no more than 5mm (¼ in) thick. Heat a wok or large pan until very hot and add oil to coat the inside.

2. Add the chicken and cook, stirring constantly, until just done. Remove to a bowl. Cook the other ingredients for the stir-fry, then return the chicken to the pan and cook for 1–2 minutes to heat through.

Roasting & carving

A roast chicken has a luxurious aroma and flavour and it makes an excellent Sunday lunch or special meal with very little preparation. To get the most out of the roast, these few simple guidelines make carving very easy, giving neat slices to serve.

Preparing the bird

1. Take the bird out of the fridge 45 minutes–1 hour before roasting to allow it to reach room temperature.

2. Before stuffing (see page 230) a bird for roasting, clean it thoroughly. Put the bird in the sink and pull out and discard any loose fat with your fingers. Run cold water through the cavity and dry the bird well using kitchen paper.

Basting

Chicken, turkey and other poultry needs to be basted regularly during roasting to keep the flesh moist. Use an oven glove to steady the roasting tin and spoon the juices and melted fat over the top of the bird. Alternatively, use a bulb baster.

How to tell if poultry is cooked

Test by piercing the thickest part of the meat – usually the thigh – with a skewer. The juices that run out should clear with no trace of pink; if they're not, return the bird to the oven and check at regular intervals. Duck and game birds are traditionally served with the meat slightly pink: if overcooked, the meat may be dry. When tested, the juices should have just a blush of pink.

Simple roast chicken

To serve four to six, you will need: **1.4–1.6kg (3–3½lb) chicken, 5 garlic cloves, 4 lemon slices, juice of 2 lemons (squeezed halves put to one side), 2 tsp Dijon mustard, 4 fresh rosemary sprigs, 4 fresh thyme sprigs, 1 sliced onion, 300ml (½ pint) chicken stock, 300ml (½ pint) dry white wine.**

1. Make incisions all over the chicken except the breast. Loosen the breast skin. Crush 3 garlic cloves and slip under the skin with lemon slices, mustard and herbs.

2. Put the lemon halves into the cavity. Put the chicken into a roasting tin. Spoon 2 tbsp lemon juice into the cavity and pour the remaining juice over. Chill for a few hours. Remove from the fridge 30 minutes before cooking.

3. Preheat the oven to 200°C (180°C fan oven) mark 6. Put the chicken, breast side down, on a rack in the tin. Add the onion, remaining garlic and 4 tbsp each stock and wine.

4. Roast in the oven for 20 minutes, turn and roast for 35 minutes or until juices run clear when the leg is pierced. Baste now and then, adding wine if needed.

5. Put the chicken on a platter and cover loosely with foil. Spoon off as much fat as possible, leaving behind the juices in the tin. Put the tin over a medium-high heat, add the remaining stock and wine and scrape up the sediment from the tin. Simmer for 5 minutes to make gravy. Strain.

ROASTING TIME FOR CHICKEN

To calculate the roasting time for a chicken, weigh the oven-ready bird (including stuffing, if using) and allow 20 minutes per 450g (1lb) plus 20 minutes extra, in an oven preheated to 200°C (180°C fan oven) mark 6.

Oven-ready weight	Serves	Cooking time (approx.)
1.4–1.6 kg (3–3½ lb)	4–6	1½ hours
1.8–2.3kg (4–5lb)	6–8	1 hour 50 minutes
2.5–2.7kg (5½–6lb)	8–10	2¼ hours

Carving chicken

After resting, put the bird on a carving board.

1. Steady the bird with a carving fork. To cut breast meat, start at the neck end and cut slices about 5mm (¼ in) thick. Use the carving knife and fork to lift them on to a warmed serving plate.

2. To cut off the legs, cut the skin between the thigh and breast.

3. Pull the leg down to expose the joint between the thigh bone and ribcage and cut through that joint.

4. Cut through the joint between the thigh and drumstick.

5. To carve meat from the leg (for turkeys and very large chickens), remove it from the carcass and joint the two parts of the leg, as above. Holding the drumstick by the thin end, stand it up on the carving board and carve slices roughly parallel with the bone. The thigh can be carved either flat on the board or upright.

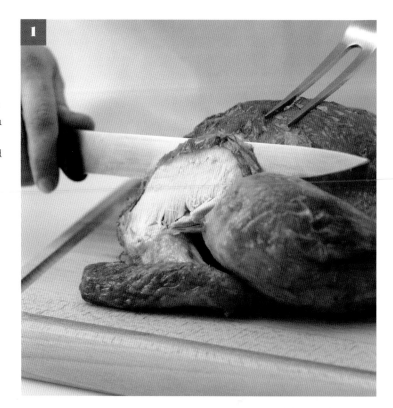

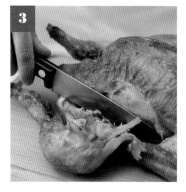

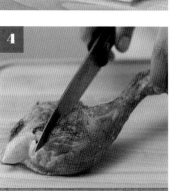

Storing leftovers

Don't forget the leftovers when the meal is finished – never leave poultry standing in a warm room. Cool quickly in a cold place, then cover and chill.

Stuffings

Some people like moist stuffing, cooked inside the bird, others prefer the crisper result when the stuffing is cooked in a separate dish – why not do half and half and please everyone? All these stuffings – with the exception of the wild rice stuffing – can be made a day ahead or frozen for up to one month. Thaw overnight in the fridge. Cook in a preheated oven, or alongside the roast.

Best-ever Sage & Onion Stuffing

To serve eight, you will need:
1 tbsp olive oil, 1 very finely chopped large onion, 2 tbsp finely chopped fresh sage, 1 heaped tbsp fresh white breadcrumbs, 900g (2lb) pork sausagemeat, 1 medium egg yolk, salt and ground black pepper.

1. Heat the oil in a pan. Add the onion and fry until soft and golden. Stir in the sage and leave to cool.

2. Put 1 tbsp breadcrumbs to one side, then mix the remainder into the sausagemeat with the onion and egg yolk. Season with salt and pepper, then leave to cool. Cover and chill overnight, or freeze.

3. Preheat the oven to 180°C (160°C fan oven) mark 4. Put the stuffing into an ovenproof dish, sprinkle with the breadcrumbs and cook for 35–40 minutes until cooked through and golden.

Sausage, Cranberry & Apple Stuffing

To serve eight, you will need:
50g (2oz) butter, 1 finely chopped onion, 1 crushed garlic clove, 4 pork sausages – about 275g (10oz) – skinned and broken up, 75g (3oz) dried cranberries, 2 tbsp freshly chopped parsley, 1 red eating apple, salt and ground black pepper.

1. Heat the butter in a pan. Add the onion and cook over a medium heat for 5 minutes or until soft. Add the garlic and cook for 1 minute. Tip into a bowl and leave to cool. Add the sausages, cranberries and parsley, then cover and chill overnight, or freeze.

2. Preheat the oven to 200°C (180°C fan oven) mark 6. Core and chop the apple and add it to the stuffing. Season and stir well.

3. Put the stuffing into an ovenproof dish and cook in the oven for about 30 minutes or until cooked through.

Wild Rice & Cranberry Stuffing

To serve six to eight, you will need:
125g (4oz) wild rice, 225g (8oz) streaky bacon, cut into short strips, 2 medium red onions, about 225g (8oz) total weight, finely chopped, 75g (3oz) dried cranberries, 1 medium egg, beaten, salt and ground black pepper.

1. Put the rice into a pan and cover with 900ml (1½ pints) cold water. Add ¼ tsp salt and bring to the boil. Reduce the heat and simmer, partly covered, for 45 minutes or until the rice is cooked. Drain and cool.

2. Heat a large frying pan. Add the bacon and dry-fry, turning from time to time, until lightly browned. Remove the bacon with a slotted spoon and transfer to a bowl. (If you have the goose liver, cook it in the same pan for 2–3 minutes, leave to cool, then chop it finely and add it to the bacon.) Add the onions to the frying pan and cook over a low heat until soft and translucent. Add the cranberries and cook for 1–2 minutes, then add the mixture to the bacon and leave to cool completely.

3. Add the cooked rice and the egg to the bacon mixture. Season, then stir thoroughly to combine. Cover and chill overnight.

4. Preheat the oven to 200°C (180°C fan oven) mark 6. Wrap the stuffing in a buttered piece of foil and cook for 30–40 minutes.

Chestnut & Butternut Squash Stuffing

To serve eight, you will need:
1 tbsp olive oil, 15g (½oz) butter, 1 finely chopped onion, 1 small butternut squash, finely chopped, 2 finely chopped rosemary sprigs, 2 finely chopped celery sticks, 1 firm pear, finely chopped, 200g (7oz) peeled and cooked (or vacuum-packed) chestnuts, roughly chopped, 2 slices – about 100g (3½oz) – walnut bread, cut into small cubes, salt and ground black pepper.

1. Heat the oil and butter in a pan. Add the onion and fry for about 10 minutes or until soft but not brown. Add the squash and rosemary and continue to cook for a further 5 minutes or until everything is soft and golden. Add the celery and pear and cook for 1–2 minutes.

2. Add the chestnuts, season with salt and pepper and mix well. Add the bread, mix everything together, then leave to cool. Cover and chill overnight, or freeze.

3. Preheat the oven to 200°C (180°C fan oven) mark 6. Put the stuffing into a buttered ovenproof dish and cook for about 25–30 minutes or until golden.

Fennel & Pinenut Stuffing

To serve eight, you will need:
75g (3oz) butter, 1 bunch of spring onions, sliced, 450g (1lb) roughly chopped fennel, 4 tbsp freshly chopped tarragon, 50g (2oz) pinenuts, toasted, 150g (5oz) goat's cheese, 150g (5oz) fresh breadcrumbs, 2 medium eggs, beaten, grated zest and juice of 1 lemon, salt and ground black pepper.

1. Heat the butter in a pan. Add the spring onions and cook for 3 minutes. Add the fennel and cook for 5 minutes, then leave to cool.

2. Add the tarragon, pinenuts, cheese, breadcrumbs, eggs, lemon zest and juice. Season with salt and pepper and mix well. Cover and chill overnight, or freeze.

3. Preheat the oven to 200°C (180°C fan oven) mark 6. Put the stuffing into a buttered ovenproof dish and cook for 30–40 minutes.

Bacon, Pecan & Wild Rice Stuffing

To serve eight, you will need:
900ml (1½ pints) hot chicken stock (see page 222), 1 bay leaf, 1 fresh thyme sprig, 225g (8oz) mixed long-grain and wild rice, 50g (2oz) unsalted butter, 225g (8oz) smoked streaky bacon, roughly chopped, 2 finely chopped onions, 3 finely chopped celery sticks, ½ Savoy cabbage, chopped, 3 tbsp finely chopped marjoram, 85g sachet sage and onion stuffing mix, 125g (4oz) chopped pecans.

1. Pour the hot stock into a pan, add the bay leaf and thyme and bring to the boil. Add the rice, cover, reduce the heat and cook according to the pack instructions. Drain if necessary, then tip into a large bowl and cool quickly, discarding the herbs.

2. Melt the butter in a large pan. Add the bacon, onions and celery and cook over a medium heat for 10 minutes until the onions are soft but not brown. Add the cabbage and marjoram and cook for 5 minutes, stirring regularly.

3. Add the cabbage mixture to the rice, together with the stuffing mix and pecans. Tip into a bowl and cool quickly.

Orange, Sage & Thyme Stuffing

To serve eight, you will need:
**2 tbsp olive oil, 1 finely chopped large onion, 2 crushed garlic cloves, 75g (3oz) fresh white breadcrumbs, 50g (2oz) toasted and chopped pinenuts, grated zest of 1 orange, plus 2–3 tbsp juice, 2 tbsp each freshly chopped thyme and sage,
1 medium egg yolk, beaten, salt and ground black pepper.**

1. Heat the oil in a pan. Add the onion and garlic and fry gently for 5 minutes until soft but not brown.

2. Put the remaining ingredients into a large bowl. Add the onion mixture and stir to bind, adding more orange juice if needed.

Rosemary & Lemon Stuffing

To serve four to six, you will need:
25g (1oz) butter, 1 finely chopped onion, 125g (4oz) fresh white breadcrumbs, 1 tbsp freshly chopped rosemary leaves, grated zest of 1 lemon, 1 medium egg, beaten, salt and ground black pepper.

1. Melt the butter in a pan. Add the onion and fry over a low heat for 10–15 minutes until soft and golden. Tip into a bowl and cool.

2. Add the breadcrumbs, rosemary leaves and lemon zest. Season well, then add the egg and stir to bind.

Falafel Balls

These stuffing balls are delicious with chicken, but are also great with pitta bread and green salad as a vegetarian meal.

To serve eight to ten, you will need:
**275g (10oz) dried chickpeas,
1 roughly chopped small onion,
a small handful of fresh coriander,
3 roughly chopped garlic cloves,
juice of ½ lemon, 2 tsp ground
cumin, ½ tsp bicarbonate of soda,
olive oil for shallow-frying, salt and
ground black pepper.**

1. Put the chickpeas into a pan and cover with plenty of cold water. Bring to the boil and boil for 2 minutes, then leave to soak for 2 hours. Drain.

2. Put the drained chickpeas into a food processor with the onion, coriander, garlic, lemon juice, cumin, bicarbonate of soda and ½ tsp salt and pepper. Whiz until everything is finely ground and beginning to stick together. Take small handfuls of the mixture and squeeze in the palm of your hand to extract any excess moisture. Shape into walnut-sized balls.

3. Heat the oil in a frying pan over a medium-high heat and fry the falafel for 3–4 minutes until they are deep golden brown all over. Drain well on kitchen paper. Serve immediately, or chill for later use.

4. To use, put the falafel into a parcel of foil and reheat alongside the roast for 15–20 minutes.

Pork, Chestnut & Orange Stuffing

To serve eight to ten, you will need:
**50g (2oz) butter, 6 roughly chopped
shallots, 4 roughly chopped celery
sticks, 1 fresh rosemary sprig,
snipped, 1 tbsp freshly chopped
flat-leafed parsley, 175g (6oz) firm
white bread, cut into rough dice,
2 cooking apples, about 225g (8oz)
total weight, peeled, cored and
chopped, 125g (4oz) cooked, peeled
(or vacuum-packed) chestnuts,
roughly chopped, grated zest of
1 large orange, 450g (1lb) coarse
pork sausagemeat, salt and ground
black pepper.**

1. Melt the butter in a large frying pan. Add the shallots, celery and rosemary and gently fry for 10–12 minutes until the vegetables are soft and golden. Tip into a large bowl. Add the parsley, bread, apples, chestnuts and orange zest to the bowl. Season and mix well.

2. Divide the sausagemeat into walnut-sized pieces. Fry, in batches, until golden and cooked through. Add to the bowl and stir to mix.

Pork, Spinach & Apple Stuffing

To serve eight, you will need:
**2 tbsp olive oil, 150g (5oz) finely
chopped onion, 225g (8oz) fresh
spinach, torn into pieces if the
leaves are large, 2 sharp apples,
such as Granny Smith, peeled,
cored and cut into chunks, 400g
(14oz) pork sausagemeat, coarsely
grated zest of 1 lemon, 1 tbsp
freshly chopped thyme, 100g
(3½oz) fresh white breadcrumbs,
2 large eggs, beaten, salt and
ground black pepper.**

1. Heat the oil in a frying pan. Add the onion and cook for 10 minutes or until soft. Increase the heat, add the spinach and cook until wilted.

2. Add the apples and cook, stirring, for 2–3 minutes, then leave to cool. When the mixture is cold, add the sausagemeat, lemon zest, thyme, breadcrumbs and eggs, then season and stir until evenly mixed.

Cranberry & Lemon Stuffing

To serve four to six, you will need:
**25g (1oz) butter, 1 finely chopped
large onion, 1 crushed garlic clove,
450g (1lb) best-quality sausages,
4 tbsp freshly chopped parsley,
2 tbsp freshly chopped sage, the
zest of 2 lemons, 1 tbsp brandy or
Calvados (optional), 75g (3oz) dried
cranberries, salt and ground black
pepper.**

1. Melt the butter in a frying pan. Add the onion and sauté for about 10 minutes or until soft but not brown. Add the garlic and cook for a further 1 minute, then transfer to a bowl and leave to cool.

2. Preheat the oven to 190°C (170°C fan oven) mark 5. Squeeze the sausagemeat out of the skins into the bowl with the onions and garlic. Add all the remaining ingredients and season, then mix well, using your hands. Shape into 18 balls and place in muffin tins or pack into an oiled baking dish and bake in the oven for 30 minutes or until cooked through and golden on top.

Marinades, spice rubs & flavoured butters

Quick & Easy Marinade

Combine olive oil, lemon or lime juice and chopped garlic, pour over chicken and marinate in the fridge for at least 1 hour.

Lemon & Rosemary Marinade

Mix together the coarsely grated zest and juice of 1 lemon with 2 tbsp freshly chopped rosemary and 6 tbsp olive oil. Pour over chicken and marinate in the fridge for at least 1 hour.

Spicy Tomato Marinade

Mix together 8 tbsp tomato ketchup with 2 tbsp soy sauce, 2 tbsp chilli sauce and 4 tbsp red wine. Add 2 tsp Jamaican jerk seasoning. Pour over chicken and marinate in the fridge for at least 1 hour.

Pineapple & Coconut Marinade

Blend ¼ peeled chopped pineapple with the scooped-out flesh of ½ a lime until smooth. Add 200ml (7fl oz) coconut milk and 1 tsp Tabasco. Pour over chicken and marinate in the fridge for at least 1 hour.

Hot & Spicy Marinade

Combine 1 crushed garlic clove, 2 tbsp ground coriander, 2 tbsp ground cumin, 1 tbsp paprika, 1 seeded and chopped red chilli (see Cook's Tips, page 8), the juice of ½ lemon, 2 tbsp soy sauce and 8 fresh thyme sprigs. Pour over chicken and marinate in the fridge for 1 hour.

COOKS TIPS

- *Use a large sealable plastic bag when marinating food: it coats the food more easily, cuts down on washing up, and takes up less space in the fridge than a bowl.*
- *Marinades will not penetrate poultry skin, so remove the skin or cut slashes in it before mixing the poultry with the marinade.*
- *Use just enough marinade to coat the flesh generously: it is wasteful to use too much, as most will be left in the base of the container. It cannot be reused once it has been in contact with raw flesh.*
- *Dry marinated meat to remove liquid from the surface before cooking. Shake off excess marinade and pat dry with kitchen paper.*
- *Pay attention when using marinades or sweet glazes made with sugar or honey, as they tend to burn if not watched carefully.*

SPICE RUBS

Sometimes referred to as a dry marinade, spice rubs are a great way to add flavour to poultry. They don't penetrate far into the flesh, but give an excellent flavour on and just under the crust. Make them with crushed garlic, dried herbs or spices and plenty of ground black pepper. Rub into the poultry and leave to marinate in the fridge for at least 30 minutes or up to 8 hours.

FLAVOURED OILS

- Look for lemon, garlic, basil and chilli flavoured oils – they can be used as a marinade. Alternatively, just brush the oil over the food before grilling.
- Even quicker are ready-made tikka and teriyaki marinades, which are perfect for most kinds of poultry.

FLAVOURED BUTTERS

A pat of flavoured butter makes an instant sauce for simply grilled chicken.
Per serving, you will need: 25g (1oz) soft unsalted butter, plus flavouring (see below).
1. Beat the softened butter together with the flavouring. Turn out on to clingfilm, shape into a log and wrap tightly.
2. Chill in the fridge for at least 1 hour. It will keep for up to one week (or freeze for up to one month).

Flavourings:

For 125g (4oz) unsalted butter.
Anchovy butter: 6 mashed anchovy fillets.
Herb butter: 2 tbsp finely chopped herbs, a squeeze of lemon juice.
Garlic butter: 1 crushed garlic clove, 2 tsp freshly chopped parsley.

Sauces

The Ultimate Barbecue Sauce

To make 300ml (½ pint), you will need:

3 tbsp olive oil, 3 finely chopped garlic cloves, 3 tbsp balsamic vinegar, 4 tbsp dry sherry, 3 tbsp sun-dried tomato paste or tomato purée, 3 tbsp sweet chilli sauce, 300ml (½ pint) passata, 5 tbsp clear honey.

1. Put the oil, garlic, vinegar, sherry, tomato paste or purée and the chilli sauce into a bowl and mix well. Pour into a pan, then add the passata and honey. Bring to the boil, reduce the heat and simmer for 10–15 minutes until thick.

Avocado Salsa

To serve four to six, you will need:
3 large ripe tomatoes, 1 large red pepper, 2 small red chillies, (see Cook's Tips, page 10) 1 finely chopped red onion, 4 tbsp freshly chopped coriander, 2 tbsp freshly chopped parsley, 2 ripe avocados, salt and ground black pepper.

1. Quarter, seed and dice the tomatoes. Core, seed and finely chop the pepper. Halve, seed and finely chop the chillies and combine with the tomatoes, peppers, onion and herbs.

2. Halve, stone, peel and dice the avocados. Add to the salsa and season well with salt and pepper. Toss well and serve within about 10 minutes. (Cut avocado flesh will discolour if left for longer than this.)

FOR QUICK SAUCES

Mango Mayo
Put the flesh of 1 large mango into a bowl and mash together with 2 tsp freshly chopped coriander, 1 tsp grated fresh root ginger and the juice of 1 lime. Season with salt and pepper. Gradually whisk in 200ml (7fl oz) sunflower oil until thick. Great with barbecued chicken.

Basil Mayo
Stir 2 tbsp basil Pesto (see Cook's Tips, page 8) into 200ml (7fl oz) mayonnaise. This is great with barbecued chicken.

Avocado Crush
Toss 1 large peeled chopped avocado in 4 tbsp lemon juice. Blend with 100ml (3½fl oz) olive oil and 2 tbsp water. Great with chicken salad.

Almond & Herb Pesto
Whiz together 50g (2oz) fresh flat-leafed parsley, 1 thick slice stale bread (crust removed), 2 tbsp lemon juice and 1–2 garlic cloves, then whiz in 50g (2oz) toasted almonds and 200ml (7fl oz) olive oil. Great with barbecued chicken.

Pastes & sauces

Ready-made pastes and sauces, consisting of ingredients such as spices, fresh chillies, onion, ginger and oil, are widely available, but most are also easily made at home.

Pastes

Harissa is a spicy paste flavoured with chillies, coriander and caraway and is used as a condiment or ingredient in North African cooking, particularly in Morocco, Tunisia and Algeria.

To make your own harissa:
Grill 2 red peppers until softened and charred, cool, then peel, core and seed.

Put 4 seeded and roughly chopped red chillies (see Cook's Tips, page 8) into a food processor with 6 peeled garlic cloves, 1 tbsp ground coriander and 1 tbsp caraway seeds and whiz to a rough paste. Add the grilled peppers, 2 tsp salt and 4 tbsp olive oil and whiz until smooth. Put the harissa into a screw-topped jar, cover with a thin layer of olive oil and store in the fridge. It will keep for up to two weeks.

Tandoori paste is used on foods such as chicken to add flavour and to give it a reddish-orange colour common in tandoor cooking.

To make your own tandoori paste:
Put 24 crushed garlic cloves, a 5cm (2in) piece fresh root ginger, peeled and chopped, 3 tbsp each coriander seeds, cumin seeds, ground fenugreek and paprika, 3 seeded and chopped red chillies (see Cook's Tips, page 8), 3 tsp English mustard, 2 tbsp tomato purée and 1 tsp salt into a food processor with 8 tbsp water and whiz to a paste. Divide the paste into three equal portions, then freeze for up to three months.

Sauces

Soy sauce – made from fermented soy beans and, usually, wheat, this is the most common flavouring in Chinese and Southeast Asian cooking. There are light and dark soy sauces; the dark kind is slightly sweeter and tends to darken the food. It will keep indefinitely.

Tabasco – a fiery hot sauce based on red chillies, spirit vinegar and salt, and prepared to a secret recipe. A dash of Tabasco may be used to add a kick to soups, casseroles, sauces, rice dishes and tomato-based drinks.

Tamari – similar to soy sauce, this fermented sauce is made from soy beans and is dark in colour and rich in flavour. Usually wheat-free.

Teriyaki sauce – a Japanese sauce made from soy sauce, mirin (a sweet Japanese cooking wine) and sugar.

Salad dressings

Balsamic Dressing

To make about 100ml (3½fl oz), you will need:

2 tbsp balsamic vinegar, 4 tbsp extra virgin olive oil, salt and ground black pepper.

1. Whisk the vinegar and oil in a small bowl. Season to taste with salt and pepper.

2. If not using immediately, store in a cool place and whisk before using.

COOK'S TIPS
- *To help it emulsify easily, add 1 tsp cold water to the dressing.*
- *To get a really good emulsion, shake the dressing vigorously in a screw-topped jar*

French Dressing

To make 100ml (3½fl oz), you will need:

1 tsp Dijon mustard, a pinch of sugar, 1 tbsp red or white wine vinegar, 6 tbsp extra virgin olive oil, salt and ground black pepper.

1. Put the mustard, sugar and vinegar into a small bowl and season with salt and pepper.

2. Whisk thoroughly until well combined, then gradually whisk in the oil until thoroughly combined. If not using immediately, store in a cool place and whisk before using.

TRY SOMETHING DIFFERENT
Herb Dressing Use half the mustard, replace the vinegar with lemon juice and add 2 tbsp freshly chopped herbs, such as parsley, chervil and chives.
Garlic Dressing Add 1 crushed garlic clove to the dressing at step 2.

Basic Vinaigrette

To make about 300ml (½ pint) you will need:

100ml (3½fl oz) extra virgin olive oil, 100ml (3½fl oz) grapeseed oil, 50ml (2fl oz) white wine vinegar, a pinch each of sugar and English mustard powder, 1 garlic clove, crushed (optional), salt and ground black pepper.

1. Put both oils, the vinegar, sugar, mustard powder and garlic, if using, into a large screw-topped jar. Tighten the lid and shake well. Season with salt and pepper.

2. If not using immediately, store in a cool place and shake before using.

Lemon Vinaigrette

To make about 150ml (¼ pint) you will need:

2 tbsp lemon juice, 2 tsp runny honey, 8 tbsp extra virgin olive oil, 3 tbsp freshly chopped mint, 4 tbsp roughly chopped flat-leafed parsley, salt and ground black pepper.

1. Put the lemon juice, honey and salt and pepper to taste into a small bowl and whisk to combine.

2. Gradually whisk in the oil and stir in the chopped herbs. If not using immediately, store in a cool place and whisk before using.

Mustard Dressing

To make about 100ml (3½fl oz), you will need:

1 tbsp wholegrain mustard, juice of ½ lemon, 6 tbsp extra virgin olive oil, salt and ground black pepper.

1. Put the mustard, lemon juice and oil into a small bowl and whisk together. Season to taste with salt and pepper.

2. If not using immediately, store in a cool place and whisk before using.

Lemon & Parsley Dressing

To make about 100ml (3½fl oz), you will need:

juice of ½ lemon, 6 tbsp extra virgin olive oil, 4 tbsp freshly chopped flat-leafed parsley, salt and ground black pepper.

1. Put the lemon juice, olive oil and parsley into a medium bowl and whisk together. Season to taste with salt and pepper.

2. If not using immediately, store in a cool place and whisk before using.

Blue Cheese Dressing

To make 100ml (3½fl oz), you will need:

50g (2oz) Roquefort cheese, 2 tbsp low-fat yogurt, 1 tbsp white wine vinegar, 5 tbsp extra virgin olive oil, salt and ground black pepper.

1. Crumble the cheese into a food processor with the yogurt, vinegar and oil.

2. Whiz for 1 minute until combined. Season with salt and pepper. Use within one day.

Chilli Lime Dressing

To make 125ml (4fl oz), you will need:

¼ red chilli, seeded and finely chopped (see Cook's Tips, page 8), 1 garlic clove, crushed, 1cm (½in) piece fresh root ginger, peeled and finely grated, juice of 1½ large limes, 50ml (2fl oz) olive oil, 1½ tbsp light muscovado sugar, 2 tbsp coriander leaves, 2 tbsp mint leaves.

1. Put the chilli, garlic, ginger, lime juice, oil and sugar into a food processor or blender and whiz for 10 seconds to combine.

2. Add the coriander and mint and whiz together for 5 seconds to chop roughly. Store in a cool place and use within two days.

Garlic, Soy & Honey Dressing

To make about 100ml (3½fl oz), you will need:

1 garlic clove, crushed, 2 tsp each soy sauce and honey, 1 tbsp cider vinegar, 4 tbsp olive oil, ground black pepper.

1. Put the garlic into a small bowl. Add the soy sauce, honey, vinegar and oil, season to taste with pepper and whisk together thoroughly.

2. If not using immediately, store in a cool place and whisk before using.

Mint Yogurt Dressing

To make about 175ml (6fl oz), you will need:

150g (5oz) Greek yogurt, 3–4 tbsp chopped mint leaves, 2 tbsp extra virgin olive oil, salt and ground black pepper.

1. Put the yogurt into a bowl and add the mint and oil. Season to taste with salt and pepper.

2. If not using immediately, store in a cool place and use within one day.

Sun-dried Tomato Dressing

To make about 100ml (3½fl oz), you will need:

2 sun-dried tomatoes in oil, drained, 2 tbsp oil from sun-dried tomato jar, 2 tbsp red wine vinegar, 1 garlic clove, 1 tbsp sun-dried tomato paste, a pinch of sugar (optional), 2 tbsp extra virgin olive oil, salt and ground black pepper.

1. Put the sun-dried tomatoes and oil, the vinegar, garlic and tomato paste into a blender or food processor. Add the sugar, if using.

2. With the motor running, pour the oil through the feeder tube and whiz briefly to make a fairly thick dressing. Season with salt and pepper. If not using immediately, store in a cool place and whisk before using.

Caesar Dressing

To make about 150ml (¼ pint), you will need:

1 medium egg, 1 garlic clove, juice of ½ lemon, 2 tsp Dijon mustard, 1 tsp balsamic vinegar, 150ml (¼ pint) sunflower oil, salt and ground black pepper.

1. Put the eggs garlic, lemon juice, mustard and vinegar into a food processor and whiz until smooth then, with the motor running, gradually add the oil and whiz until smooth.

2. Season with salt and pepper, cover and chill for up to three days.

Classic Coleslaw Dressing

To make about 175ml (6fl oz), you will need:

2½ tbsp red wine vinegar, 125ml (4fl oz) olive oil, 1 tbsp Dijon mustard, salt and ground black pepper.

1. Pour the vinegar into a screw-topped jar. Add the oil and mustard and season with salt and pepper. Screw on the lid and shake.

2. Combine with the coleslaw ingredients and chill until needed.

Chilli Coleslaw Dressing

To make about 100ml (3½fl oz), you will need:

½ tsp harissa paste (see page 238), 100g (3½oz) natural yogurt, 1 tbsp white wine vinegar.

1. Put all the ingredients into a small bowl and whisk to combine.

2. Combine with the coleslaw ingredients and chill until needed.

Index

Leabharlanna Poiblí Chathair Bhaile Átha Cliath
Dublin City Public Libraries